Go Birdi

'The pleasure of studying
birds, and the pleasure of
finding out new things, can be
combined at small cost in
money, though more in time, by
anyone so inclined.'

DAVID LACK, *THE LIFE OF THE ROBIN*, 1943

GO BIRDING!

Introduced and edited by Tony Soper
Illustrations by M. J. Loates

BBC BOOKS

This book accompanies
the BBC Television series
Go Birding!,
first shown on BBC 2
in 1988.

Series produced by
George Inger and Robin Prytherch
and presented by Tony Soper.

Published by BBC Books
a division of BBC Enterprises Ltd
Woodlands, 80 Wood Lane, London W12 0TT

First published 1988

ISBN 0 563 20650 0

Set in 10 on 13pt Palatino by
Redwood Burn Limited, Trowbridge, Wiltshire
Printed and bound in Great Britain by
Redwood Web Offset, Trowbridge, Wiltshire

CONTENTS

THE CONTRIBUTORS

TONY SOPER has been associated with the BBC's Natural History Unit since its beginnings, first as a film producer but more recently as a freelance writer and presenter. He has been involved with a long string of BBC wildlife programmes.

DR PATRICK THOMPSON graduated from Paisley College in 1981 and moved to Liverpool Polytechnic, where he carried out postgraduate research on the breeding biology of Redshank. He joined the BTO in March 1987 to analyse the BTO's long-term Garden Bird Feeding Survey data and to carry out further studies on the importance of gardens for birds.

DR DAVID WINGFIELD GIBBONS is presently organising the *New Atlas of Breeding Birds in Britain and Ireland* for the BTO. Prior to this he completed a PhD on brood parasitism in Moorhens at Cambridge, and carried out research on Jackdaws and damselflies in the Camargue, southern France.

PETER GRANT is an editor of the influential magazine *British Birds* and was chairman of its rarities panel. An expert in bird identification, he is an enthusiastic twitcher.

DR MIKE MOSER graduated from Durham University and started his ornithological career in the Camargue, southern France, where he carried out a PhD study on herons. He joined the BTO in 1982 as Estuaries Officer, and was appointed Director of Development in 1986.

DR ROBERT PRŶS-JONES studied British buntings for his PhD, and subsequently spent extended periods researching birds in the Seychelles, Australia and South Africa. He is currently the Estuaries Officer of the BTO.

CHRIS MEAD has worked for the BTO for twenty-six years. He is in charge of the National Bird Ringing Scheme and has personally ringed about 250 000 birds. Chris is also a well-known broadcaster and author.

BOB SCOTT is the Senior Reserves Manager of the RSPB and is much involved with the problems of international bird conservation.

List of Illustrations

List of Diagrams

Charts and graphs by Mike Gilkes   Maps by Alan Burton
* by M. J. Loates

Picture Credits

BTO page 107 (Chris Mead)
MANSELL COLLECTION page 104
RSPB pages 108, 113 (C. H.
    Gomersall), 162–3 (Acroyd
    Photography).

The photographs on the front cover
and page 76–7 were taken for the
BBC by George Inger.

INTRODUCTION

Tony Soper

Birds are arguably the most enjoyable of our fellows on this planet. Like us, they sing and dance in pursuit of rewarding relationships with each other. They come in all colours, shapes and sizes, they live wherever there are signs of life, from the polar regions to the deserts and the seas. Some live solitary lives, some prefer to gather in enormous flocks, some alternate between the lonely life and the gregarious one, much as we do. Unlike most wild mammals, they tend to be creatures of daylight, depending heavily on their senses of sight and sound – again much as we do. So although there are profound differences between our ways and their ways, the similarities make for a fellow feeling which draws us close to the birds.

For all that, they enjoy one facility which is forever denied to us: they can fly by their own unaided efforts. And it has to be this one marvellous power which makes their behaviour so fascinating. The annual migration of Swallows from the insect-rich northern summer to the tropical Africa which merely sustains them through the 'winter' is remarkable enough, but there are plenty of other examples of feeding movements in which birds take advantage of changing local conditions. If the ash mast crop fails, Bullfinches will ravage the orchards for early buds; if a cold snap freezes eastern Britain, then there will be a mass exodus to the milder west and we'll see Whooper Swans in Devon.

Most birdwatchers seem to become hooked on the activity by way of the garden bird table before they move on to the heady pastures of estuary and cliff face, to say nothing of the delights of island-hopping. And one of the continuing pleasures of birding is that it can be pursued anywhere, through the kitchen window, the office window (I have my desk turned to the wall because I know that if I look out of the window there will be Cormorants fishing for dabs and Curlews excavating for lugworms and just maybe a Greenshank passing by . . .), from the train window or on just about any excursion anywhere for any purpose. So it is impossible for life ever to become boring if you are a birder!

But sooner or later you will want to share both your interest and your observations with others. One of the astonishing phenomena of the last few decades has been the growth in membership of the Royal Society for the Protection of Birds, which has so effectively taken up the challenge of adapting to a rapidly-changing world. With a continuing programme of education and reserve creation and management, the RSPB leads the world in showing how man and bird can co-exist and even flourish. For although there are plenty of things to be despondent about, there are also plenty of examples in which birds are improving their prospects as we approach the turn of the century. Ospreys and Avocets are rapidly becoming two a penny, Kestrels hunt the motorways and Collared Doves arrive practically out of the blue and successfully colonise Britain. Birds and birding are dynamic subjects and there will never be a lack of interesting ornithological problems to solve. Cetti's Warbler may have established itself, but what will be the next bird to grace the British List?

What is the convert to this most rewarding activity to do with the nuggets of information he collects? For, make no mistake, every day will bring some new observation, even if it is only the number of Blue Tits visiting the bird table. The answer is to join the ranks of those who make sure their birding makes a useful contribution to ornithological science. Join the RSPB to underpin the work of that indispensable organisation, but then join the British Trust for Ornithology in order to take part in the surveys and census work which are at one and the same time so time-consuming and so enjoyable.

In this book we explore the many ways in which casual observation can transform itself into the pursuit of knowledge! Serious it is, but solemn it doesn't have to be, and I can say with my hand on my heart that birders are good company . . .

1

FOOD AND FEEDING

Patrick Thompson

All birds must eat and drink to live. The amount of food required to satisfy the demands of a bird varies greatly depending on the size of the individual, the area in which it lives, the type of food being consumed, the time of year and of course many other factors. A Blue Tit, for example, must eat more during very cold weather than on a warm summer day to compensate for energy used in keeping itself warm. And in the breeding season birds must greatly increase their feeding rates when they have a nest full of hungry young. So it is fair to say that most species vary their diet and the amount of food consumed to meet their everyday energy requirements.

HOW BIRDS FEED

At the most general level, birds may be divided into those which eat animal matter and those which eat plant material. Of the animal eaters, there are those which eat live prey and those which only feed on dead matter (carrion). Many birds which feed on animal matter also eat some vegetable matter. The range of vegetable foods eaten is almost endless – fruits, buds, nectar and seeds of numerous kinds. Whether plant or animal, all foods must provide the bird with the nutrients (protein, fats, carbohydrates and vitamins) that it requires to live. Just like people, birds require a mixed diet to remain healthy and functional.

HOW BIRDS DIGEST THEIR FOOD

All animals have a digestive system of varying complexity. Basically, large units of food must be broken into small units which can then be transported throughout the body to the regions where they are required. In birds the digestive system is fairly sophisticated. To put it in simple terms, the digestive system consists of an entry point (beak and mouth), the oesophagus (neck) and crop, stomach and the intestine. When the bird eats some food it passes into the system and then is broken down. To gather their food, all birds have beaks which are adapted to suit the type of food they eat – for example, finches have beaks which can crack open seeds while waders, which dig for marine worms, have delicate probing beaks. Many birds have a crop. No digestion takes place in the crop, but, rather, it is an area where food can be temporarily stored before digestion. In the Greenfinch for example, the crop is well developed allowing the finch to eat a large amount of seed material quickly. It may then retire to a safe place to digest the food. This adaptation allows these birds to feed more efficiently at less risk to themselves.

Other birds fill their crops before settling down to roost at night. In our bitterly cold winters, this food can then be broken down to supply the energy essential to maintain body temperature throughout the night.

From the crop and oesophagus, the food passes into the stomach. In many mammals, the food has already been partly broken down when it reaches the stomach. However, birds have no

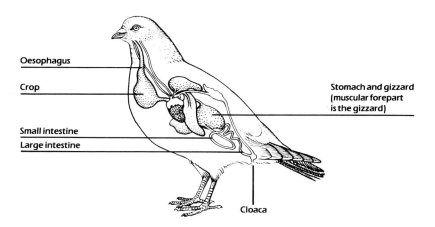

Oesophagus

Crop

Stomach and gizzard
(muscular forepart
is the gizzard)

Small intestine
Large intestine

Cloaca

teeth with which to break up food and, although some birds can use their beaks to break the food up to a small extent, the food normally enters the stomach fairly intact.

Many carnivorous birds produce powerful acids in their stomachs which rapidly break the food into manageable units. In other birds, the food must be physically broken down, in a special compartment within the stomach, called the gizzard, before the digestive acids can begin to act. The gizzard is the muscular forepart of the stomach. Here, muscular contractions break up the food into smaller pieces. However, this is still not enough to break up the hardest of food items. To improve the efficiency of the gizzard, many birds eat stones and grit which help to grind down the tougher food parcels. Examination of a dead bird known to feed on vegetable matter will often reveal a gizzard containing stones of various sizes.

Once broken down sufficiently, the food enters the main part of the stomach, where it is chemically broken down. The material then passes into the intestine where the necessary nutrients are absorbed into the blood system for transport throughout the body.

In those birds which eat large amounts of vegetable matter, the intestine is greatly distended to enable materials to be absorbed more efficiently. The length of the entire gut system is constrained by the fact that the bird must be able to fly. A lengthy tract would be heavy, impeding the bird's ability to fly. Grouse, for example, consume large amounts of vegetable matter, and consequently the gut is very long. Not surprisingly Grouse are not particularly strong flyers, preferring to fly in short bursts.

From the intestine the remaining material passes out of the body as faeces. The faeces may be dry or wet depending on the availability of drinking water. In those birds which live where water is not readily available, much of the water is recycled thereby conserving a precious resource.

ADAPTATIONS TO FEEDING METHODS

The adaptations which birds have evolved to capture or obtain their food are almost as varied as the range of foods they eat. Even within a family of birds, many different feeding techniques may be used. At the species level, it is possible to compare the different methods employed and to see how these best suit an individual's life style.

PETRELS

The petrels are superbly adapted for life at sea. They spend hours on end soaring above the waves, only coming to dry land to breed. The Manx Shearwater has a well-developed crop which allows it to store large quantities of its fish prey. The fish are captured near the water surface and swallowed into the crop whole. Because shearwaters have short legs, they are vulnerable when they come to land. As a consequence, they only come to their nesting burrow at night to feed

their chick. Therefore it is of great benefit to be able to carry a large amount of food for the solitary nestling. Shearwaters make good use of this crop; British breeding shearwaters have been recorded transporting food from the bay of Biscay to their nesting colonies off the west coast.

WILDFOWL

Wildfowl are one of the most diverse groups of birds found in Britain. They obtain their food in a wide variety of ways. Some ducks, such as the Shelduck, gather food from mud which they sieve through their beak. Others, such as Wigeon, graze aquatic and estuarine plant life. Geese also nibble grasses which are broken down in a long gut system. The grazing wildfowl have short broad bills which are ideal for grasping short grasses. Ducks such as the Eider have a more powerful beak which allows them to eat prey such as mussels and crabs, whilst the sawbills (mergansers and goosanders) have slender bills with serrations. The serrations allow them to grip fish which they capture by diving under water.

Different beaks for different feeding techniques:
TOP Shelduck, Pinkfoot, Red-breasted Merganser.
BOTTOM Wigeon, Eider.

Ducks also exhibit various feeding behaviours to obtain their food. Some species, such as sawbills, dive for fish; others, such as Shovelers and Shelducks, paddle in the muddy shallows filtering sediment whilst some upend in shallow water and pull up weeds and other aquatic plants. This is characteristic of birds such as the Mallard and Mute Swan. Clearly feeding behaviour and feeding structures are intricately linked.

BIRDS OF PREY

One of the most spectacular groups of birds are the raptors, birds of prey. They specialise in eating both live and dead prey. Prey is normally captured by the feet and then torn apart by a sharp hooked bill. The Golden Eagle eats both live prey (birds and mammals) and carrion (typically dead sheep or deer). The prey is held on the ground in the huge talons and the bill used to break up the quarry. Smaller birds of prey, such as the Kestrel and Hobby, are not so powerful but are very skilled hunters. The Kestrel has the ability to hover whilst searching for its prey (typically small mammals). The falcon drops on its prey capturing it, and usually killing it instantly, with its feet. The Hobby catches much of its prey in mid-air. These dashing falcons are marvellous fliers, able to capture aerial insects and even the fast-flying Swifts in the air. The smaller items of prey may be consumed on the wing.

Carrion specialists such as the vultures spend hours on the wing searching for dead animals. These birds require enormously powerful beaks to tear open the hide of some of the larger land mammals. These birds often go for days without food so when they do find it they gorge themselves almost to the point where they are incapable of taking to the air.

Hobbies are falcons which hunt in fast direct flight.

The food eaten by some birds has been identified by examination of pellets. Many birds produce pellets – bundles of undigested food which are regurgitated through the mouth from the stomach. Pellets are an important research tool for birdwatchers in that they can be broken up and analysed to discover what food has been eaten.

How to dissect pellets

Pellets can be dissected when either old or fresh. Place the pellet in a shallow tray of warm water to soften the structure. The pellet can then be teased apart using needles or forceps and the constituents identified. Many amateurs have dissected owl pellets to discover what foods have been eaten. Owls, like other birds of prey, are not able to digest bone. The pellet will therefore often contain teeth, bones and skulls as well as other undigested material such as beetle shells. Pellet analysis is great fun and can easily be carried out at no great cost. Pellets can be found underneath roost sites of birds like Kestrel and Tawny Owl, but it is also possible to find wader and gull pellets along the shoreline where these birds have been roosting.

GAME BIRDS

Game birds like the Grouse and Pheasant are primarily vegetarians. They have short but powerful bills to nip off the tops of buds, shoots and stalks. Typical of vegetarians, their diet varies seasonally depending on what is available; indeed they will even eat some insects in the summer. The digestive tract is long to handle the large amount of material ingested, and grit is eaten in large amounts.

WADERS

Waders illustrate the wide variation in feeding adaptations which can exist within birds of the same family. The bill structure of each species of wader is highly adapted to enable the bird to obtain a particular type of food.

The Oystercatcher, for example, has a powerful bill which it uses to remove and open mussels found on the coast. But within the species, some Oystercatchers specialise on estuarine mudflats feeding on worms. These individuals have longer, more pointed, bills.

The Avocet has a long upturned bill. This bird wades through deep water, moving its bill from side to side. As it moves the highly sensitive bill discovers tiny shrimps. Plovers like the Lapwing have short legs and short bills. These birds feed on invertebrates such as earthworms and leatherjackets which are located and pulled clear of the soil.

Perhaps the greatest range of feeding adaptations is demonstrated by the sandpipers. Members of this family have legs and bills of varying lengths. Small sandpipers such as the Little Stint have short legs and a very short bill. Larger members such as the Dunlin have longer legs and a downcurved bill. The Curlew Sandpiper's bill is even more curved, making it ideal for probing for small invertebrates in soft mud and sand. Larger sandpipers like the Greenshank have longer legs and a longer more powerful upturned bill, whilst the Curlew has an enormous bill and very long legs. The leg length is important in the sandpipers in that longer-legged individuals are able to hunt in deeper waters. Equally, a long bill makes it possible to reach prey which a short-billed bird could not reach. The waders are a perfect example of how feeding structures are perfectly adapted to suit an individual's needs in specific habitat. The variety and form of specialisation also means that different birds normally hunt and feed in different areas, thus reducing competition for food between species.

GULLS

Gulls are opportunists and their numbers have increased greatly in the latter half of this century as a result of an increase in organic wastes both on land and at sea. At sea the gulls have cashed in on the wastage from the trawling industry, whilst on land they scavenge on refuse tips picking out any organic material.

FISHING BIRDS

Specialist ocean fishers such as the auks have highly adapted beaks for catching and holding fish. The colourful Puffin sometimes dives to great depths to capture fish. During the breeding season, captured fish are held in the bill and then taken to the nesting burrow. Like the shearwaters these birds are vulnerable when they come to land. As a consequence, they carry as many fish as they can manage to take to the nest on each trip.

The Kingfisher is a superb fisher. It perches above a stream or canal and, on sighting a suitable prey, dives beak first into the water, capturing the fish between the mandibles. This technique is quite different from that of our other spectacular fishing bird, the Osprey. The Osprey captures its prey by diving feet first into the water and grasping the fish by the claws. Other birds which dive from above the water for fish include the terns and the Gannet. Interestingly some birds, even though they are not closely related, have evolved the same behaviour to solve the problem of obtaining prey.

INSECT HUNTERS

Some of our summer migrants such as the Swift and Swallow are superb fliers which hunt the skies for aerial insects. The Swift, which only lands to breed (it even roosts on the wing), catches all its prey with a gaping bill whilst flying. Locally these birds may be found feeding in large numbers above a thermal or other spot where aerial insects have been concentrated.

NIGHT FEEDERS

Some of our birds, such as Tawny Owls and Long-eared Owls, are almost entirely night feeders. These birds have superb night vision and acute hearing which allows them to locate small mammalian prey moving around on the ground. Once located, prey is captured in the owl's sharp claws and torn up by a very sharp bill. In contrast, the Nightjar feeds on aerial invertebrates. Like the Swift, it captures its food by gaping the bill and scooping up any insects encountered.

WARBLERS

Many of our summer migrants are members of the warbler families. Most warblers have a varied diet. Some specialise on invertebrates (mainly arthropods), whilst others feed on insects and fruits. All warblers have small bills and much of their feeding is done while moving amongst twigs, branches, leaves etc.

FINCHES

The finches are another group of birds which, like waders, are frequently used to demonstrate the range of feeding adaptations which can arise. In Britain, several species of finch can be seen in the garden. The variety of bill structures and the way in which they are used demonstrate the very fine relationship which exists between an animal and its diet. Finch beaks vary from the fine bill of the Linnet to the heavy structure of the Hawfinch. In all finches, the bill is modified internally for holding and shelling seeds. The bill is often used for extracting seeds from the seed heads of plants (particularly so in Greenfinch, Goldfinch, Crossbill and Siskin). The large powerful bill of the Hawfinch is used for crushing large hard tree-fruits. Goldfinches and Siskins have longer but thinner tweezer-like bills which

Variety of bill structures in the finch family:
TOP Hawfinch and Linnet. BOTTOM Bullfinch and Crossbill.

are used for probing and removing seeds from seed heads such as thistles and ragwort. The troublesome but very handsome Bullfinch has a rounded bill which is used for eating buds whilst the Crossbill has a special bill which is used to extract the seeds from conifer cones. As we shall see later, the diet can be quite different during the winter months when some natural foods are in short supply. Although the seed-eating finches also feed insects to their young, their digestive tract, like their bill, is particularly well adapted to a seed diet. Large quantities of seeds may be held in the gullet from where they may be regurgitated either for their own consumption or to be fed to their chicks. Many finches are social, choosing to feed in small flocks wherever seeds may be found. Frequently these birds will feed a long distance from the nest thereby making a food pouch an essential extra for efficient feeding.

CROWS

The crows have a diet which is almost as varied as their bill structures. Most of the crow family appear to be fairly opportunistic, feeding on almost any food found. The Raven has a heavy bill which is used for feeding on carrion. The bill of the Carrion and Hooded Crow is smaller but nonetheless strong. Other crows such as the Jay and Magpie can regularly be seen in country and suburban gardens. Although both are frequently accused of destroying the nest of every breeding garden bird, it seems that eggs and young make up only a small part of the diet. Rooks spend much time foraging in agricultural land for invertebrates and will take some vegetable matter.

WHY SO MANY WAYS OF FEEDING?

The variety of ways in which birds feed is remarkable. However, all animals must feed if they are to live and to do this they must exploit a foodstuff which will not put them in direct competition with other species. The solution to this problem lies in the vast array of beak and leg structures and behaviour patterns which allow each species to specialise on particular types of food or in particular habitats.

WATCHING BIRDS FEED

Birds feed in a variety of ways and are superbly adapted to obtain or capture their food as efficiently as possible. Many of the birds which have already been highlighted are to be found away from the more populated areas, but there are many more which can regularly be seen feeding at close quarters.

IN TOWN

The Feral Pigeon is familiar to all of us. This bird is descended from the Rock Dove which is now rarely found along the remote western coasts of Britain, inhabiting sea cliffs and coastal mountain cliffs.

Now completely at home amongst the flats and office blocks of the town centres, the Feral Pigeon has adapted to a new way of life. On a day-to-day basis, the pigeon feeds on any scraps which it finds in park pavements or on the roadside.

Other birds can also be seen at close quarters in a town centre. The House Sparrow, like the Feral Pigeon, has discovered that towns offer a regular supply of food. In the country House Sparrows still have a more traditional diet, feeding on seeds, grains and invertebrates. During the winter months, they regularly attend bird tables where they will feed on almost anything. Their preferred foods are nuts, seeds and table scraps. They learn very quickly how to collect foods from what are to them unnatural feeding positions and it is not unusual to see them clinging to a nut bag whilst extracting a nut with their sturdy bill. Although they normally feed on the ground, the Sparrows have adapted their feeding method and behaviour to suit the environment, so that they are now one of the most widespread of species. Whilst House Sparrows are by no means the most colourful of birds, they are rewarding to watch and are very interesting in that they have adapted their life styles so successfully.

An equally successful urban bird is the Starling. Starlings are known to everyone by their magnificent iridescent spotted plumage. Outside the breeding season, Starlings form enormous flocks when they fly in to roost on the window ledges of town and city centres. A flock of one hundred thousand Starlings is a spectacular sight and the noise generated as they settle down for the night is considerable. Obviously a large flock of birds concentrated in such a small area is a major problem because they produce a tremendous amount of droppings. The scale of this problem is considerable, and many city councils know only too well the cost of cleaning and maintaining buildings which are regularly used by roosting Starlings.

Normally Starlings can be seen feeding in small flocks on short grass in playing fields, parks or on the lawn. They move across the grass surface probing their long bill into the turf as they move. Although they normally feed on insects and other invertebrates, Starlings also rely on bird-table food during the winter. At the bird table they are aggressive and frequently drive away other birds or at least make them wait until they have finished. You should be able to attract these birds very easily and will find that they take a wide range of foods.

IN THE GARDEN

Blackbirds are also common visitors to suburban gardens, where the variety of shrubs provides them with nesting cover and a rich and varied food supply. These birds are not as adventurous as Sparrows or Starlings and normally prefer to take their food from flat surfaces such as a table or the ground. Just as some birds prefer to feed on a particular food, some birds like to take their food in a particular way. Anyone with a garden or access to a garden can observe this for themselves by providing food for the birds.

Bird Feeding Stations

Try starting off with a table and several hanging units. If you provide a number of different foods in different ways you should attract a variety of birds. Within a few days you should be able to appreciate that some birds will try anything and will attempt to take food from any position whilst other birds are less adventurous. Whilst the Sparrow takes all the foods from all the feeding units, the Blue Tit only feeds from the hanging units. You will also notice that some birds appear to be present all the time whilst others appear less regularly and feed intermittently. Finally, a simple feeding station can also highlight the fact that some birds are more frequently recorded than others. Whilst generalisations of this sort are dangerous, the exercise does make it clear that some birds are more numerous or more visible than others. Whether you are watching a Great Tit feeding on hanging nuts, a Robin feeding on the bird table or a Blackbird feeding on scraps on the ground, you will soon appreciate that birds (like people) have favourite foods.

ON MOTORWAY VERGES

Other birds may be encountered in our day-to-day lives. Anyone who has driven along a motorway will surely have seen a Kestrel hovering at the roadside. They hunt along the road verges because the grass is normally kept short, making it easier for them to spot their prey – small mammals and insects. Other birds such as the Rook and Carrion Crow may also be seen feeding at the roadside.

The Rook prefers the short grass verges in which to hunt for its invertebrate prey; whilst the Carrion Crow, as its name suggests, feeds on any birds or animals which have been hit by the fast-moving traffic.

AT THE LOCAL RESERVOIR, LAKE OR BOATING POOL

You can often see ducks and swans here. The beautiful Mute Swan, once so common in many parts of the country, has declined in recent years as a result of lead poisoning. These swans inhabit areas of water which also happen to be the favourite spots for coarse fish and angling. Over the years, many anglers have lost their tackle which often includes several pieces of split lead to add weight to the line. Mute Swans feed on aquatic vegetation which they gather from the water by submerging their head and neck below the water surface. Whilst consuming this food, some swans also ingest lead weights which then lie in the gullet as would grit. From here, tiny amounts of the lead enter the swan's body leading to death in the most extreme cases. As a result of this poisoning, the Mute Swan has disappeared from many of its former haunts. The vast majority of anglers enjoy watching the wildlife which inhabits their local fishing grounds. Indeed, many angling clubs are responsible for the management and protection of some of our more interesting waterways. With the co-operation of these clubs, it is hoped that anglers will soon become more aware of the problems they are causing and take steps to use non-toxic fishing weights.

BIRDS IN CONFLICT WITH MAN

Many people may find it difficult to recognise that bird feeding behaviour is of any relevance to our way of life. Whilst feeding, however, many birds come directly into conflict with man. To understand how such conflict can be avoided, it is important to understand why the conflict arises.

In agriculture and horticulture there are many birds which are recognised as pests. Perhaps the most well-known garden pest is the Bullfinch. Bullfinches are specialists, feeding for part of the year on buds – in particular, the buds from fruit trees. In some years, the damage caused to trees in both domestic gardens and orchards is so great that the yield is noticeably reduced; indeed, the crop may fail almost completely. Whilst the Bullfinch is a beautiful bird, this is small compensation to the gardener or farmer.

Other birds conflict with man's food-growing industries. Ripe cereal is pulled down and eaten by Woodpigeons, Sparrows, Rooks and some finches. The losses may not be large, but the farmer must still set up bird-scaring equipment to minimise them. Birds also feed on newly planted crops, but this damage is normally less serious.

In some parts of the country, wintering geese have become a serious problem. In particular, geese have been recorded in Britain feeding on carrots, potatoes, turnips and brassicas. Although they normally graze estuarine grasses, geese have also caused some damage to winter cereals and spring pastures. In the spring, any loss of grass can be considerable because this is the time when a farmer's stored foodstuffs are at their lowest and when livestock need fresh grass. When a problem occurs it is often serious as geese flocks in this country are often recorded in tens of thousands. Geese seem to favour areas which are sufficiently large and quiet to allow them to feed and roost in peace. Where possible, therefore, it seems that setting up sanctuaries within the major geese wintering areas may be at least a partial solution, allowing the geese to feed quietly and safely.

The aquaculture industry has also reported cases where bird feeding has conflicted with their activities. Anyone who has an outdoor fish pond may have had fish stolen by a Heron. On a much larger scale, Herons have become considerable pests on trout fish farms, taking large numbers of fish. Other birds, such as the Cormorant and the Osprey, have also learned that these areas offer a rich

supply of fish. Whilst the Osprey is very rare, with only fifty pairs nesting in Britain, Cormorants and Herons are relatively abundant. To a fish farmer the loss of fish could be considerable, reducing profits and the efficiency of the business. The only solution has been to cover the pools with wire mesh.

Shellfish farms have also been attacked, particularly by Eiders. These diving ducks can eat a considerable number of mussels and oysters, and can cause damage to the growing apparatus. The fish farming industry is relatively new, so it is likely that other birds will discover and cash in on this food source.

For sporting reasons, man is also responsible for the management of the country's fish and game stocks. Grouse, Pheasants, Partridges and game fish are maintained in order that the sporting rights can be leased as a commercial venture. Other fish-eating birds clash with the interests of man in this area. In particular, the Red-breasted

Merganser and Goosander are blamed for the decrease in salmon stocks. There is no doubt that these birds do feed on young salmon and trout, but there are almost certainly many other important factors involved in the decline of the fish stocks of many rivers.

Similarly, birds of prey such as the Hen Harrier and Peregrine have been blamed for the decline in Grouse stocks on our moors. The result has been that both birds of prey and the fish-eating sawbills have been hunted down and destroyed almost wherever they occur. Not surprisingly, many people feel that this is at best a misguided attitude and at worst a deliberate act of vandalism with absolutely no justification. Whilst the level of this persecution has fallen over the last few years, it is still at a significant level in some areas. Clearly, without a full understanding of a species' requirements and dietary intake, it is unfair to blame all reductions on natural predators.

Finally there are cases whereby a bird's feeding habits may endanger man's life. Large flocks of birds moving to roost or moving from the roost to the feeding grounds are a considerable hazard to jet aircraft. Airports troubled by birds have employed a variety of techniques to scare these birds or to prevent them coming near the area. A number of mechanical bird-scaring devices have been used as well as some more natural ones. Some airports have employed falconers to fly falcons over the airstrip. The presence of these birds of prey keeps away many of the smaller flocking birds such as Starlings.

In recent times, some of our larger gulls have taken to feeding on municipal refuse tips where large amounts of organic waste are dumped. These birds also frequently congregate on areas of water (sometimes a reservoir) where they preen and roost. Whilst on the water the birds frequently defaecate, spreading organisms from their gut into the drinking water. Gulls were suspected of spreading salmonella from refuse tips to drinking water in Strathclyde (Scotland). Clearly the potential for the spread of bacteria is quite large. Large gatherings of birds at sensitive places need to be closely monitored.

GARDENS AS A BIRD HABITAT

Over the years, many changes have taken place in our countryside, greatly reducing the area and diversity of habitats. In particular, agricultural practices have changed enormously with a resultant change to the countryside. Hedges have been cleared, fields have become bigger, mixed farming has declined, the use of chemical fertilisers has greatly increased and the number of people working in farming has fallen rapidly so that many rural areas which were traditionally farming are now in decline. The resulting change in the face of our countryside has led to the decline and local extinction of many of our farmland birds.

There has also been a great reduction in the amount of deciduous woodland in the last century. Although there has been massive reafforestation in many areas, there has been a tendency to plant coniferous trees rather than the slower-growing (and therefore less commercially viable) hardwoods. Many of our woodland birds have suffered declines similar to the farmland birds.

And it does not stop there! Other habitats such as marshland and heathland have also been greatly reduced, decreasing the diversity of habitats to be found.

Against this background of habitat destruction and change, there has been a steady increase in the land area occupied by industrial development and private housing. The area covered by gardens is now twice as large as the total area of all our national nature reserves. Gardens are therefore becoming increasingly important as a bird habitat.

In 1970, the British Trust for Ornithology (BTO) set up the garden bird feeding survey (GBFS) in order to determine how important gardens are as a bird habitat and how individual species were dependent on gardens. It was hoped that we would learn more about feeding patterns and food preferences, and that the survey would also stimulate people to take more interest in the birds around them. By taking part in the GBFS, the amateur ornithologist can make a considerable contribution to our understanding of bird feeding biology.

THE GBFS

The survey is now entering its eighteenth year. Participants provide food and water for the birds and record the bird numbers on a weekly basis from the beginning of October to the end of March. The participants must have good identification knowledge of birds and be prepared to watch their garden whenever possible. Many of the most dedicated members are housewives and retired people who find the survey fulfilling and enjoyable. No time limits are attached to the period of observation for the survey.

On any week that observations are made, the watcher must record only those birds which come to the supplied food or water. The birds are counted whenever the garden is watched; at the end of the week, the highest 'peak count' for each species is recorded on the survey recording sheets. The 'peak count' is the number of birds of each species seen feeding and drinking at any one time. All observations are made within a defined area of the observer's garden and those birds feeding on natural foods are not recorded. The observers must also specify how their food is presented in order that analysis may determine how much of each food was available. In addition, they must keep a note of unusual behaviour, and weather information.

At the end of each three-month period, the observers return their forms which, depending on the garden locality, are grouped into rural and suburban. All the data are then stored on a computer at the BTO headquarters in Tring and analysed. Although the survey was originally set up to look at the range and numbers of birds using gardens during the autumn and winter period, we have also learnt an enormous amount about feeding methods and times.

BRITISH TRUST FOR ORNITHOLOGY - GARDEN BIRD FEEDING SURVEY

Site Registration Number . . .

TABLE A1 - WEEKLY BIRD COUNT

Please record PEAK COUNTS only for each week as explained
in the instructions. No additions or averages please.

Winter 1987/88, week beginning- and week number;

Office use only	Species;	OCT 4- 1	OCT 11- 2	OCT 18- 3	OCT 25- 4	NOV 1- 5	NOV 8- 6	NOV 15- 7	NOV 22- 8	NOV 29- 9	DEC 6- 10	DEC 13- 11	DEC 20- 12	DEC 27- 13
1	BLUE TIT													
2	ROBIN													
3	BLACKBIRD													
4	HOUSE SPARROW													
5	STARLING													
6	DUNNOCK													
7	CHAFFINCH													
8	GREAT TIT													
9	GREENFINCH													
10	SONG THRUSH													
11	COAL TIT													
12	PIED WAGTAIL													
13	COLLARED DOVE													
14	WREN													
15	MISTLE THRUSH													
16	B-HEADED GULL													
17	MAGPIE													
18	MARSH/WILLOW TIT													
19	JACKDAW													
20	GT.SP.WOODPECKER													
	*													
	*													
	*													
	*													
	*													
	*													

Record of feeding units' positions

HANGING													
TABLE/ RAISED SURFACE													
GROUND													

* Additional spaces are for species not named in list.

THE BASIC BIRD TABLE

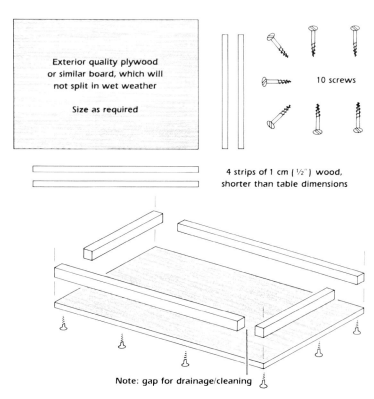

Exterior quality plywood or similar board, which will not split in wet weather

Size as required

10 screws

4 strips of 1 cm (½″) wood, shorter than table dimensions

Note: gap for drainage/cleaning

HANGING TABLE
Nylon cord or light metal chain and screwing eyes, one at each corner

TABLE ON A POST
2 or 4 small metal brackets at top and pegs to hold base

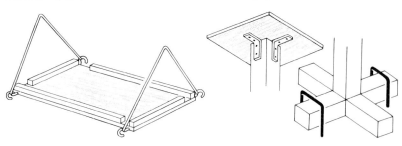

Extra nails and hooks for hanging nut bags or wire baskets

HOW TO PRESENT THE FOOD

Birds will feed on almost any food presented in almost any way. Certain foods, however, are more attractive and, when presented properly, a wide range of species can be encouraged to visit the garden.

A general word of warning must be made here. If you live in an area where a large variety of birds does not occur naturally, then no end of food or bird tables will make any difference to what you can attract. If you live in an inner city area where only a few bird species are to be found, then it is unlikely that you will attract a large variety of birds. However, you may attract large numbers of a few species which have enormous appetites. So when you are buying or building feeding units, try to envisage what birds you might attract.

As a rule, birds will feed on almost any type of feeder as long as they can get at the food easily. Some species must take their food from a flat stable surface; but for others, the feeding unit can be hanging. Bird-table design is now almost as complex as bird behaviour. Basically, all that is required is a flat surface with a rim to prevent food falling off and thus being wasted. Birds tend to squabble so it is best to have several tables thereby reducing the load on any one table. The squabbling will never stop, but it will allow some of the less aggressive birds to get at the food.

If you want to attract a number of different species, then it is best to provide food in a variety of ways. In addition to a bird table, it is always advisable to supply some food on the ground as some species like the Dunnock prefer to eat from the ground. Other species such as the Blue Tit normally feed from small twigs and therefore prefer to take their food from a hanging feeder. There are now many different hanging feeders available for your garden. Many are expensive but, of course, this does not mean they will attract more birds!

WHAT FOOD TO PUT OUT

Peanuts (unsalted) should be placed in a hanging wire mesh feeder, the mesh size being large enough to allow the birds to extract whole nuts. Many birds will feed on nuts so it is advisable to scatter some on a flat surface as some birds will also eat nuts off the ground as well as from a bird table. Other foods such as fat and fat mixes (a mixture of seeds and fruit set in melted fat) may be presented in hanging tit bells. The tit bell may be any cup-shaped object which can hold

ABOVE AND TOP RIGHT Fat and fat mixes are poured into a cup-shaped receptacle such as a small flower pot and left to set. The bell is hung from a string, providing an invaluable food supplement.

BELOW Conventional hanging feeders.

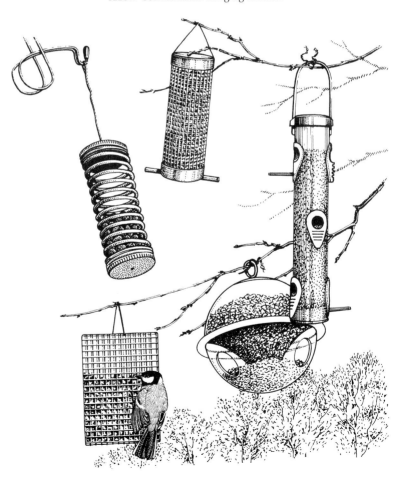

melted fat until it is set. The bell is then hung in a suitable position, allowing only those birds which feed whilst hanging upside down to feed. The important thing to remember is that food should be offered on a regular basis. Birds quickly become dependent on provided food, so don't provide a huge amount one day if you cannot provide a similar amount the next! It is better to provide a small amount of food every day. You will soon learn that certain species spend more time on one food type than on others. Many species have particular preferences for both the type of food and the way it is presented.

PROVIDING WATER

Every garden which intends feeding birds should also provide drinking water. Like food this can be provided in a variety of ways, although it must again be emphasised that birds will drink from any water device that is accessible to them. During very cold weather when most water is frozen, birds need water just as much as food.

WHERE TO POSITION YOUR FEEDING STATION

Feeding and drinking devices can be placed in a variety of positions. The first and most important consideration when siting a bird table must be for the birds' safety. Generally, the feeding units should be positioned within two to three metres of cover. However, the cover should not be so near the feeding units that a hungry cat can creep up and pounce on the birds, giving them no time to escape. Aerial predators such as the Sparrowhawk may also be attracted to large concentrations of feeding birds. Whilst it is never nice to see one of our feathered friends killed, it is nonetheless breathtaking to see a hawk at close quarters taking a small bird and, even with the best of intentions, there is very little you can do to prevent it.

FINDINGS OF THE GBFS

FAVOURITE FOODS

Some species feed on many foods showing no real preference, whilst others are specialist feeders concentrating on several types. The general feeders include the Starling, Robin and Pied Wagtail. All these species take a wide variety of foods. To an extent, the House Sparrow will also eat almost anything, although it does seem to prefer nuts – especially when these are provided on the ground.

The GBFS has shown that nuts are the preferred food of many species. The Blue Tit, Coal Tit, Greenfinch, Great Spotted Woodpecker, Great Tit, Nuthatch and Siskin all prefer nuts when provided. Other birds prefer to feed on seeds of various types. The Bullfinch, though not a very common garden visitor, prefers to feed on small seeds as do the Brambling and Chaffinch. In recent years, however, both Brambling and Chaffinch have shown an increasing tendency to feed on nuts from the ground (although only rarely from a hanging feeder). Goldfinches are also attracted to seeds – especially balm and teazle seeds. Although a nut specialist, the Greenfinch also feeds extensively on seeds, especially sunflower seeds. The other small finches such as the Redpoll and Linnet are not recorded frequently in gardens; but when they are, they are normally to be found feeding on small seeds. Buntings, such as the Reed Bunting and Yellowhammer, also prefer seeds. In some very cold winters, these birds come into gardens in quite large numbers but normally they are casual visitors.

Collared Doves and Woodpigeons feed largely on grain and seeds. These birds can be aggressive, often driving away other birds attempting to feed in the area. As in the case of an aggressive thrush, the only solution seems to be to spread the food around thus giving other birds a chance to feed in peace.

Apart from the Blackbird, members of the thrush family prefer to feed on fruit of many types and condition. Both the Redwing and Fieldfare are attracted to apples. Mistle Thrushes are also attracted to fruit during cold weather. These large thrushes are very aggressive in defence of their food, often spending much of the day driving off other thrushes. Blackbirds prefer fruit of a variety of types but will also eat many other foods – nuts, fats, seeds, bread and, of course, table scraps. Other birds which prefer to feed on fruits are the Blackcap and the Green Woodpecker. Until recently, Blackcaps were rare garden visitors in winter, preferring to migrate to warmer climes in southern Europe and North Africa. Since 1950, the number of Blackcaps wintering in Britain has steadily increased. Although still an unusual winter visitor, these birds are becoming more regular. When they do occur, they prefer fruit, especially chopped apples. Green Woodpeckers are not frequently recorded feeding in gardens but, when they are recorded, it is often on windfall apples.

Many species eat fat – presumably because it provides so much energy and is relatively easy to extract. Although many species utilise this food source, the only species which seem to prefer it to other foods are the tiny Goldcrest and the Treecreeper. Treecreepers are very fond of suet and can be attracted by spreading this on the tree trunks in the garden.

Perhaps the most unpopular garden visitors are the gulls and crows. All the crows apart from the Raven and Chough are regularly recorded feeding in gardens. These birds will eat almost anything and almost any amount where it is provided. Most crows are naturally wary of human presence, so the best way to reduce the number of crows feeding in your garden is to site your feeders reasonably close to your house. The Magpie is the one bird which perhaps more than any other is frequently chastised by GBFS participants. Within garden bird circles, it is generally accepted that Magpies cause more damage to nesting birds than almost anything else. Whilst there is no doubt that Magpies do sometimes find and rob nests, such food items make up only a small proportion of their diet. In recent years there has been an increasing amount of Magpie criticism. It may well be that Magpies are subtly changing their feeding habits as they are increasing in numbers.

SHOULD WE FEED WILD BIRDS?

Many birds can be enticed to come into gardens, particularly when the weather is very cold with freezing temperatures and snow. At such times the provision of food is important allowing many birds to feed in relative ease and perhaps increasing their chance of surviving the winter. Clearly, the number of birds using gardens suggests that many birds find this source of food very important.

It has been argued that birds should not be fed during the winter months because this may allow some birds to survive which would otherwise die. Whilst this may be true, one must also realise that bird habitats have and are continuously being changed by man's activities to the detriment of many populations. While feeding birds in your garden could never redress the imbalance we have caused, only the most heartless could advise against such feeding.

HOW DO NEW FEEDING PATTERNS EMERGE?

Until recently, several species such as the Siskin, Brambling and Greenfinch were irregular garden visitors. Over a period of time, these birds learned that food was available in gardens and that the food could be obtained at a low energy cost. How do such learning patterns emerge? In the case of the Siskin, it seems that birds first turned to gardens as a source of food when the alder crop, on which they normally rely, failed. The Siskin was first reported taking food from bird tables in 1961. Since then, Siskins have become frequent visitors to gardens, with up to forty per cent of GBFS gardens recording them. It has also been established that Siskins tend to return to the same wintering area each year so it is not too difficult to see how a chance behaviour pattern could be passed on. As Siskins are social birds normally feeding in flocks, young birds of the year could and do feed in a flock which contains some experienced individuals thereby benefiting from the experiences of the older birds. New

Siskins have learnt to exploit the food sources provided in suburban gardens.

birds would therefore have followed the more experienced birds into the gardens when their natural foods were exhausted. It is conceivable that this happened in several areas quite separately and has therefore resulted in the rapid change in feeding patterns which we have seen.

Another classic example of how a feeding habit can spread in a population concerns the removal of milk bottle tops by members of the tit family. This practice was first recorded in Hampshire in 1929 but thereafter spread quickly to several areas. It seems that several individuals discovered – presumably by chance – that cream was to be found on the top of milk bottles. Thereafter, the habit spread rapidly, presumably as a result of birds watching individuals which had already acquired this skill.

Although our understanding of bird feeding preferences in gardens has been greatly advanced by the GBFS, our knowledge of natural food preferences is very much poorer. The study of feeding is difficult and for many species we have only a sketchy knowledge of which foods are preferred. Nonetheless, the work of the GBFS has been important – not least because it has also helped us establish which birds enter gardens to feed and drink.

Since 1970 no less than 133 bird species have been recorded feeding in gardens between 1 October and 31 March. Some of these species are recorded in almost every garden, whilst others are recorded only rarely. Because the survey was designed to record peak bird counts, it has been possible to look at bird numbers on both a week-to-week basis and on an annual basis. The results show how the use of a garden changes throughout the winter and between winters.

Further to this, in 1987 many participants were involved in an extension of the GBFS from April to the beginning of June, giving us an insight into the use of artificial foods during the breeding season.

MOST FREQUENT GARDEN VISITORS

The birds most frequently recorded in gardens between October and March are in descending order as follows:

Blue Tit	House Sparrow
Blackbird	Dunnock
Robin	Great Tit
Starling	Song Thrush
Chaffinch	Coal Tit
Greenfinch	Collared Dove

In the winter of 1985–86, Collared Doves were recorded on at least one occasion in seventy-four per cent of all gardens covered. Other species are recorded less frequently but are nonetheless important members of the garden community. The most abundant birds in gardens are the House Sparrow and the Starling.

The numbers of birds in gardens fluctuates for each species, and the following section looks at some of the more important garden birds and how their use of gardens changes throughout the winter and spring. Different species are dependent on gardens at different times and for a variety of reasons.

The Robin, Dunnock, Blackbird, Blue Tit and Chaffinch may be present in your garden all the year round, yet during the winter months, their numbers may increase dramatically. Indeed, although it may appear that only five or six Blue Tits are present at any one time, many more may use the garden both on a daily and annual basis. Experienced bird ringers normally expect to catch ten times as many Blue Tits in a garden as are counted on any one occasion. Clearly, by feeding the birds in your garden you are supporting many more birds than perhaps realised.

Another striking example of this problem of counting is demonstrated by Greenfinches. In some locations, the peak count for these birds at any one time has been recorded as less than 100; yet at the end of the season up to ten times more birds may have been captured in the same garden. Many of these birds are simply passing through, but it is also true to say that many feed over a wide area, entering a large number of gardens for a short period of time.

Apart from a few residents, the majority of birds feeding in your garden during the winter have migrated from less suitable wintering habitats. Some, such as the Fieldfare and Redwing, appear on a fairly regular basis from Fennoscandinavia and Iceland; whilst others undertake local migration perhaps from a neighbouring woodland or, in the case of Reed Buntings, from nearby wetlands. To highlight several of the more significant movements which take place, some of the GBFS index figures are reproduced overleaf.

For each species, rural and suburban gardens have been separated to allow the reader to consider the relative levels of bird species in each type of garden.

HOUSE SPARROW

A very common garden bird regarded by many as a pest. These birds are normally found living in close association with man and they are great opportunists, eating almost anything. At the start of the survey, House Sparrows were recorded in seventy-one per cent of rural gardens and eighty-six per cent of suburban gardens. These birds were recorded from more gardens in the spring than at any other time. If we look at the GBFS House Sparrow index, we see that sparrows were recorded from a high percentage of gardens throughout the survey. Like the Starling, the House Sparrow was more frequently recorded in suburban than in rural gardens. Whereas many birds stop feeding on bird-table foods during the spring, House Sparrows continue to feed on these foods often alongside their fledged young.

BLUE TIT

Blue Tits were regularly recorded in both suburban and rural gardens. Between eighty-three and ninety-seven per cent of all gardens reported Blue Tits well into April. From late April, Blue Tits began to leave gardens, returning to the woodlands from which they came. There is a clear build-up in tit numbers over the winter period, followed by a sharp decline from March onwards. Many Blue Tits undertake local movements from woodland to garden areas during the winter period. As the majority of rural gardens are surrounded by some woodland, it is not surprising that rural gardens support larger numbers of tits than suburban gardens.

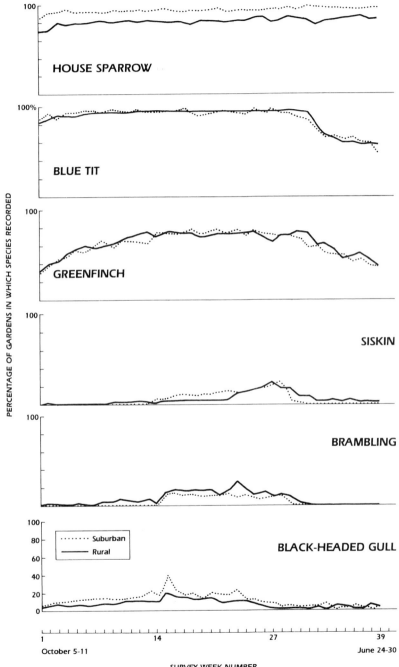

HOUSE SPARROW

BLUE TIT

GREENFINCH

SISKIN

BRAMBLING

BLACK-HEADED GULL

······ Suburban
—— Rural

PERCENTAGE OF GARDENS IN WHICH SPECIES RECORDED

October 5-11

June 24-30

SURVEY WEEK NUMBER

GREENFINCH

The gregarious Greenfinch frequently enters gardens to feed on nuts and sunflower seeds. Like the Blue Tit, it tends to be recorded in higher numbers in rural than suburban gardens but is just as likely to be seen in either garden type. The Greenfinch is naturally a seed eater, so its food is scarce in late winter and early spring. Not surprisingly, these finches tend to be recorded in gardens well into the spring. Over the duration of the GBFS, they have been coming into gardens earlier each year. Many of these birds now rely heavily on nuts and the habit of bird-table feeding has spread quickly – presumably because, like Siskins, Greenfinches return to the same wintering area each year.

SISKIN

Since the early 1960s, Siskins have become more frequently recorded in gardens. The Siskin breeds in much of northern Britain, and many of the birds which appear in gardens in the south of the country are migrants from the north and from central Europe. They only enter gardens after natural food sources have been exhausted. They move out of gardens at the end of the winter, with most birds leaving suddenly in the space of a couple of weeks. Because of the tendency to feed as a flock, there is a dramatic increase in the weekly peak counts when the birds arrive from their breeding grounds. Like many of our migrant visitors, these birds are recorded infrequently some winters.

BRAMBLING

This species is an even more erratic visitor to our gardens. In some years when their natural food (beechmast) is scarce these birds undertake mass migrations until they find suitable food. As the availability of beechmast is not normally regular, these beautiful birds may winter in completely different areas from one year to the next.

OPPOSITE Sample results from 1986–87 GBFS.

Those birds which are seen in British gardens are normally from Fennoscandinavia. Although they normally arrive in Britain fairly early in the winter, they are often not recorded in gardens until late December or January. Often, a period of cold weather is enough to bring them in, and they quickly adjust their habits to feed on nuts and seeds. The return migration does not normally begin until the end of April or beginning of May. It will be interesting to see if Bramblings increase their use of gardens in the coming years. It is probable that the infrequent nature of their appearance will make this unlikely.

BLACK-HEADED GULL

Like a few of the other birds, the Black-headed Gull only comes into gardens in extreme cold weather. Many birds flood into gardens during prolonged periods of cold weather with sub-zero temperatures. Black-headed Gulls are great opportunists and, like the House Sparrow, will eat almost anything that is loose and lying on a flat accessible surface. During the 1986–87 GBFS recording period, these gulls were recorded most frequently in both garden types during week 15 of the survey. (Many other species such as Redwing, Fieldfare, Reed Bunting and some of the commoner garden species also peaked during this week of cold weather.) Black-headed Gulls tend to leave their feeding areas only when food becomes scarce or unavailable. Many of these birds feed on earthworms; during periods of cold weather, the ground is frozen forcing the gulls to leave the pastures in search of other more available prey. They may then become a serious nuisance to other, smaller feeding birds.

By watching and recording the birds feeding and drinking in gardens, the GBFS participants have made a significant contribution to our understanding of garden bird numbers and feeding habits. The GBFS is still operating and it is intended that this survey should continue to run for the foreseeable future. The long-term aim is to study annual trends in bird numbers and to monitor changes which are taking place in the use of gardens in this country by birds. As the GBFS has been running for such a long time, it is hoped that it will be possible to detect actual changes in bird populations by looking at the number of birds using gardens – although this is, perhaps, only applicable to the commoner garden birds.

As part of the garden bird project, the BTO is now running a new garden bird survey sponsored by BASF. The new survey is a year-round exercise intended to study bird numbers and habits on a seasonal basis. This survey is designed for mass participation and it is hoped that when it concludes we will have discovered which birds are dependent on gardens for breeding and migration stops as well as for overwintering.

BEHAVIOUR WHILE FEEDING

The study of bird behaviour is both complex and fascinating, offering the amateur ornithologist great opportunities to learn much about birds and at the same time have a lot of fun.

PECKING ORDERS

Within most groups of animals there are recognised pecking orders which have been established over thousands of years. These pecking orders are nature's way of ensuring that the minimum of physical aggression is required by an individual to exert its authority over another. Birds are no exception to this rule. Wherever birds are found feeding on limited amounts of food (for example, a single feeder filled with nuts), there will be competition. Where there is competition, the existence of a pecking order or rank system allows individual species and birds to feed more efficiently, therefore improving the chances of all the birds present getting some food. Males are often dominant over females and older birds dominant over young birds.

Pecking orders exist both between species and within a species. In any garden where food is available but not in enormous quantities, some species will be more dominant than others and therefore feed before, and often for longer, than less dominant individuals. Birds like the Magpie, Mistle Thrush and Collared Dove are very aggressive in defence of food and will frequently spend a large amount of time attempting to drive away all-comers. Where only a small amount of food is available, they may successfully defend the resource until they have satisfied their requirements. However, where food is liberally scattered, this aggression may not be sufficient to deter all birds. When food is naturally in short supply, this type of behaviour is recorded more frequently. It is also true to say that the plight of the less dominant individuals is greater at such times and they could therefore be expected to be more determined in their efforts to feed.

Amongst the smaller birds, the Starling reigns supreme followed by the House Sparrow. At a hanging nut feeder it is not unusual to see birds queueing up waiting their turn to feed. In many areas Sparrows now feed quite successfully from hanging feeders, forcing Greenfinches (which are, in their own way, quite aggressive birds) to wait. The Great Tit is more aggressive than the Blue and Coal Tit, but less so than the Greenfinch and so the order of rank has been established.

FEEDING HABITS

Watching birds feeding also allows the observer to see at close hand the relationships between species and to learn more about feeding habits. Some species are superbly adapted for feeding from branches on buds and fruiting bodies. These species take readily to hanging feeders, whereas those which normally feed on the ground are less able to do so. Some species (such as the Greenfinch) normally feed as a flock, whereas others (such as the Nuthatch) are often more solitary. We have already seen that some birds have wide dietary preferences whereas others tend to be very specialised preferring perhaps one or two food items. This can be simply demonstrated if you are prepared to spend a little time and money setting up your garden so that you offer a range of foods in a variety of ways.

Gardens offer unique opportunities for individuals interested in wildlife to learn and appreciate better how birds live from day to day. Competition, migration, food chains, food choice, energy requirements, seasonal abundance, habitat choice and natural selection are all demonstrated easily by watching garden birds in garden habitat. Students of biology and ecology all agree that it is much easier to appreciate principles when they can be demonstrated and observed at first hand rather than relying on the blackboard and textbook. Whilst it is true to say that a garden is not the only place where most of these can be observed, it is difficult to think of anywhere that is more accessible.

2

NESTS AND NESTING

David Wingfield Gibbons

GREAT AMATEUR BIRD NESTERS

Edgar Chance could have been forgiven for expecting Mary Pickford to lay her eggs in the morning. After all, even in 1918 it was well known that most species of bird laid their eggs early in the morning. Mary Pickford, however, was no ordinary bird. She was one of Chance's population of Cuckoos and, as Chance went on to discover, Cuckoos lay their eggs in the afternoon. With the wisdom of hindsight, the reason for this is clear. Cuckoos do not build their own nests, rather they lay their eggs in the nests of other species, and in Britain these host species are most commonly the Meadow Pipit, the Reed Warbler and the Dunnock. Should a female Cuckoo lay in a nest before the host female herself has laid, this could lead to desertion of the nest by the host. To ensure this does not occur, the Cuckoo waits for the host female to lay her egg in the morning, then, whilst the host is absent in the afternoon, removes the host's egg and replaces it with her own. Chance, however, spent an entire year patiently watching Meadow Pipit nests in the mornings before, quite by accident, he realised his mistake.

Over a four-year period immediately after the Great War, Chance followed the daily fortunes of a handful of Cuckoos and their Meadow Pipit hosts on a local heath. He came to know one particular Cuckoo so well that, by manipulating the nesting cycles of the unfortunate Meadow Pipits, he could predict exactly when and where she would lay her eggs. He even persuaded a well-known cinematographer to record the laying procedure, and the resulting film was

Cuckoos lay their eggs directly into the nest of the foster parent.

shown to members of high society in London to rapturous applause. In so doing, Chance was not only making ornithological history by unravelling the Cuckoo's secret (as he called it), he was also performing some of the first field experiments with birds.

Despite Chance's obvious flair for bird study, he was an amateur ornithologist, undertaking all his observation and experiments in his spare time.

Some twenty years later another (perhaps less well-known) amateur, Lieutenant-Colonel Ryves, was undertaking what is now seen as a classic study of the Corn Bunting at a site in north Cornwall. With the help of his wife, Ryves's painstaking observations showed, to the mind of most, that the male Corn Bunting was outrageously polygamous. In some cases, one male would have up to four wives, making it, at that time, the most polygamous of European songbirds. (Recent research has shown that it has been usurped by the Fan-tailed Warbler.) During two field seasons, Ryves faithfully documented the lives of twenty-five males and their harems, and he came to know the territory-owning males as, in his own words, '. . . a man knows each individual of his dog team'.

Unfortunately, Ryves never attempted to catch and individually mark (with colour rings) his Corn Buntings and so, strictly speaking, he could never prove the extent of polygamy but only guess at it. Because of this lack of proof, some ornithologists refused to take his work as seriously as it merited, and Ryves was done a great disfavour when his work was more or less forgotten.

One of these dissenters was the century's most acclaimed ornithologist, David Lack. In his classic work *Ecological adaptions to breeding in birds*, Lack doubts Ryves's evidence of polygamy. Whilst Lack was strictly correct in doing this, current research has vindicated Ryves's findings.

Many think of Lack as a giant among professional ornithologists, yet forget that for the first thirty-five years of his life he was an amateur, doing much of his fieldwork during his holidays from school and university, and later in his spare time whilst a master at Dartington Hall School. For many of us, it is already too late to emulate Lack's achievements, as he began his first intensive study of birds at the precocious age of eight, and had written his first scientific paper by the time he was in his first year at Cambridge. Whilst at Dartington, Lack undertook a detailed study of a colour-marked population of Robins, thus avoiding the criticisms aimed at Ryves. This work culminated in the production of a book *The Life of the Robin*, the success of which propelled him into the public's eye, and eventually on to become the first director of the respected Edward Grey Institute of Field Ornithology at Oxford.

Neither Chance nor Ryves had any formal training in zoology or ornithology. Yet, with a good deal of common sense, a love of natural history and a patient eye, they were, like Lack, able to produce classic works on the nesting habits of their chosen species. Should they so choose, any birdwatcher could mimic the achievements of these three great ornithologists. But without a sound understanding of nesting biology, and a knowledge of a few tricks of the trade either to find nests or persuade birds to nest in accessible places, this task becomes inordinately more difficult. The aim of this chapter is to point would-be Chances or Lacks in the right direction.

NESTING

It could be argued that reproduction is the reason for the existence of a bird. Everything a bird does – eat, avoid being eaten, sing, defend its territory or migrate – is ultimately aimed at a single goal: successful reproduction. For many this goal is elusive. Fulmars often have to wait for eight years before they can attempt to breed, and the vast majority of fledgling Great Tits die before they even have the chance. Breeding is not an easy matter, and can prove costly for a bird. Female Pheasants not only starve themselves whilst incubating, as they rarely leave the nest, but they are also sitting targets for predators like foxes.

For a typical songbird, the breeding cycle begins in the late winter or early spring of each year with the male proclaiming his ownership of a territory by singing at its boundaries, in an attempt to repel all other males and to attract a mate. As soon as the male finds a mate, he sings much less. This is taken to the extreme in the Sedge Warbler which ceases singing altogether, hence the short song-period of this species. In yet other species, the female actually chooses her mate on the basis of the song; female Great Tits prefer males with complex songs to those with simple songs.

After a few days the female begins to build a nest, and the male will take this as his cue to begin guarding his mate from the amorous advances of neighbouring or unpaired males. This is because the female is most fertile at this period, and no male would wish to rear offspring which he had not fathered. Once the female begins to feather the lining of the nest, egg-laying is not far away. Most species of songbird lay a single egg a day in the morning. During the laying period, which lasts a few days, the female may well only visit the nest occasionally, preferring to feed in order to build up the reserves needed to complete the clutch. Incubation, in which the female (and often the male) exposes her brood patch to the eggs, may begin before completion of the clutch, although the precise timing of this varies greatly between species. The incubation period of songbirds is generally about twelve days to a fortnight, although the female may well leave the nest a number of times each day in order to feed. In some species, for example the Robin, the male will also help during this period by bringing food to the female and feeding her on, or near to, the nest. The period from hatching until the chicks reach independence, which is divided into the nestling and fledgling phases, is unquestionably the most exhausting period of a bird's life. During this stage, the adult bird has to fly to and from nest or fledgling, feeding its hungry brood hundreds of times a day. A number of experiments have shown that increasing the parents' work load, by giving them a few extra chicks, lowers their chance of surviving the winter: clear evidence of the cost of rearing chicks. After a period of about a month (two weeks in the nest and about the same out of it), the chicks are independent, and the parents are free to start another brood. Occasionally the female may begin laying her second clutch while the male takes care of the first brood alone.

OPEN-NESTING AND HOLE-NESTING

The nesting habits of birds can be broadly divided into two categories: those species that nest openly, such as Blackbirds, and those that nest in holes (generally in trees), such as Great Tits. Both strategies have advantages and disadvantages. Hole-nesting species are saved from the time-consuming process of building strong, elaborate nests which will safely hold their clutch and brood. Furthermore, hole-nesters are much safer from predators, as access to the nest is so restricted – just a simple hole through which the parent bird and its brood can squeeze. Given these apparent advantages, it is not always clear why any species should nest openly. There is, however, one very big disadvantage of hole-nesting: the availability of nest-holes is limited. As with the housing market in southern England, desirable residences are in remarkably short supply, especially for first-time buyers. This leads to competition for nest-holes, a time-consuming business from which the open-nester is saved; it can build its nest, within limits, wherever it chooses.

Some hole-nesting species, such as Kingfishers and Woodpeckers, have surmounted this problem by digging their own nests. However, most are only capable of modifying existing holes, or accepting them as they are.

A simple experiment has shown that the availability of nest-holes is limited. In a wood near Oxford, all suitable nesting holes were owned by territorial pairs of Great Tits. The surplus of the population were forced to live in the surrounding hedgerows (a much less favourable habitat, with very poor nesting sites), and consequently reared fewer young. By trapping and removing the woodland residents, a number of nest sites became available, and the hedgerow birds deserted the poorer habitat in favour of the woodland, where their breeding success improved.

The pros and cons of open versus hole-nesting are much more complex than this. David Lack was one of the first to point out the great difference in egg size and clutch size between open and hole-nesting species. Anybody who has seen a clutch of Blue Tit eggs in a nest-hole cannot fail to be impressed by the tiny size of the eggs and their enormous number (ten is not uncommon). Because chicks of open-nesting species are particularly vulnerable to predators (their begging calls often give them away), a parent should want to reduce the time the chick spends in the nest as much as possible. One way of doing this is to lay large eggs, with plenty of reserves, such that the chicks hatch at a relatively advanced stage of development. A female who lays large eggs can only lay a few eggs. Because of this, open-nesters tend to lay a few large eggs, whilst hole-nesters tend to lay many small eggs.

Another aspect of nesting biology that is common to hole, but not open-nesters, is that due to the competition for nest sites, some females are forced to lay their eggs in another bird's nest. Such behaviour is called *brood parasitism* or *egg dumping*, and it is now becoming clear that many hole-nesting birds (for example, Starlings and many of the cliff and bank dwelling martins) have to suffer the cost of rearing chicks that are not their own.

Surprisingly, perhaps, many species of duck are hole-nesters, sometimes nesting high up in holes in trees; and brood parasitism is common in these species. Because of the unusual pattern of dispersal and migration from the breeding grounds, mother and daughter ducks often end up nesting alongside one another. Although it remains to be proved, daughters may well 'parasitise' the nests of their mothers when nest sites are limited and the inexperienced daughters (those first-time buyers) are unable to find their own holes. In this case, the mother may be more of a willing participant than an unfortunate (and unknowing) host, as it will enable her to rear a few grandchildren, which otherwise might not exist, alongside her own brood.

The lack of suitable nest-holes can be turned to great advantage by the ornithologist, because he or she can make artificial nest sites simply by putting up nest-boxes. To the amateur ornithologist, there is a clear advantage in choosing to study a species that can be persuaded to nest in a box. The nest can be placed in a position where it can both be visited easily, and the nest contents examined quickly, with minimal disturbance to the nesting pair.

FINDING NESTS

Most of us have probably seen only a handful of birds' nests in our lifetime. The same could not be said of Arthur Whitaker who, over a period of sixty years (1889 to 1949) spent scouring the countryside around Yorkshire and Derbyshire, found over 21 000 birds' nests belonging to 180 species. His meticulous notes have provided us with a wealth of knowledge about birds' nests and how to find them.

Searching for, and finding, nests can be an absorbing hobby. It requires a mixture of delicacy, skill and patience, and can produce the thrill of finding a previously undiscovered nest. However, at the onset, it should always be made clear that nest searching for its own sake can be not only damaging – in terms of disturbance to the nest and its surroundings – but is also, for some species, downright illegal. The nests of a number of rare species (Schedule 1 species) should not even be approached, much less visited, without the necessary permission from the government. Furthermore, before anyone considers searching for nests, they should always have a good reason; either to ring the brood, or as part of a detailed study of a bird population, or in order to submit their observations to the 'Nest Record Scheme' of the British Trust for Ornithology (see p. 58). Failing this, nests should be left well alone.

There are essentially two techniques for finding nests. One is to search for the nest yourself, the other is to let the parent bird give away its nest site. The first of these, sometimes called 'cold searching', relies upon a knowledge of the precise nesting requirements of the species under consideration. Once the type of nesting habitat and typical nest position are known, the habitat is searched exhaustively during the breeding season and nests are more or less stumbled upon.

A typical example of cold searching would be looking for Jackdaw nests. This is a hole-nesting species that is as much at home in crevices in cliffs and buildings as it is in holes in trees. Being a hole-

Suitable nest holes are hard to come by. Jackdaws defend them.

nester, nest sites are in short supply, and once a pair has a hole of its own, they guard the hole year round – even during the winter. Finding Jackdaw nests is thus simple. Locate a suitable colony (by looking for flocks of birds circling above the colony), and check every hole that is Jackdaw-sized or larger (these will not be as common as you might think). A quick sniff of the nest is enough to tell you whether the hole is occupied, as Jackdaws have a very characteristic odour which is easily learnt.

To quote Bruce Campbell, an expert nest finder, 'Success in cold searching goes to those who spend the longest time looking in the largest number of likely places; it is a question of persistence rather than of skill or scientific observation'. Whilst, on the whole, this is true I would suggest that the skill comes in the form of knowing the 'likely places', and this knowledge only comes from experience in the field.

Another technique that can be added to the arsenal of the cold search is the 'rope-drag', whereby a rope is dragged between two observers over vegetation in which, it is suspected, nests are to be found. The idea is to flush the sitting bird. The rope is then laid gently on the ground, and the area where the bird flushed from is searched. This technique is used for species that nest on the ground in thick cover. Although the technique may seem crude, it is not as risky to the nest and its contents as might be thought, as the vegetation invariably keeps the rope well off the ground. For some species of wader, such as the Snipe, this is often the standard technique used for finding nests. However, it is only recommended for professionals or very experienced amateurs.

A number of species, in particular game birds like the Woodcock and Red Grouse, will often refuse to flush from the nest. It is quite possible to be straddling the nest of a Woodcock, and still not see the female. The only answer here is to use either trained dogs or thermal imaging equipment, the former using the smell, and the latter the body heat of the sitting female to give away the presence of the nest. Needless to say, these techniques can prove expensive.

Woodcocks sit tight on the nest.

A lot of time and effort can be saved whilst nest searching if the territory boundaries of the species in question are known. The reason for this is that once a nest is found in a particular territory, there is no point searching that territory further (unless bigamy is suspected). Whilst this can save a lot of effort in nest searching, working out the territory boundaries can be equally time-consuming. However, this in itself can be enjoyable, and involves simple mapping of male song posts and boundary disputes, much as used in the British Trust for Ornithology's Common Birds Census.

The second method of finding nests involves considerably more skill, as it relies upon following adults back to their nest, and is thus more appealing to many birdwatchers. This technique is best used during the nest-building and chick-feeding stage, as the parents carry nest-material and food back to the nest at regular intervals. All that is required is patience and a little luck.

This techique, however, is clearly only suitable for species that build nests and feed their young. Ducks and game birds do not fall into this category. They invariably lay their eggs in a simple feather-lined scrape, and the chicks, once hatched, feed themselves with little help from their parents.

Once a site has been located it may prove impossible to see into the nest. The answer to this problem is to construct a nest-mirror – a stick or telescopic pole with a small mirror (with a wide angle of view) attached to it via a ball-joint. A nest-mirror is particularly useful for seeing into the nests of open-nesters at medium heights (two to five metres). Finally, a torch may well prove invaluable when trying to peer into nest-holes.

CARE WHEN VISITING NESTS

The number of visits to a nest should be kept to a strict minimum – just sufficient to give the information required. Two parts of the nest cycle are very sensitive to disturbance: the laying/early incubation period, and the period just prior to fledging. A bird which has just begun laying or incubating has invested very little time and energy in the brood, and if the disturbance were great enough might be prone to desert and re-nest. Later in the nesting cycle, for example when young chicks are in the nest, a parent would be much less will-ing to desert as it had already invested much, and might not be able to re-nest. The period just before fledging is similarly sensitive, not because of fears of parents deserting the brood, but for fears of the brood deserting the nest in a single 'explosion'. If a nest is visited a day or two before fledging, all the chicks may explode from the nest at a premature age. This is an adaptation against predation as it may be better for a chick to jump from the nest, and have a small chance of survival, than to stay in the nest and be eaten for certain. Exploded chicks have a very low chance of survival, and even if they can be found it is extremely difficult to fit them back into the nest, although this can be done with more success for hole-nesters.

A final note of caution is to respect not only the nesting birds, but also their surroundings. If you cut or crush vegetation to get to the nest, Crows, Magpies and other egg thieves will also be able to get at the nest much more easily. Repeated visits also increase the chance that the local Crows will get to know the nest site, as they are notoriously good at learning to follow humans.

NEST-BOXES

Despite all these hints on how to find nests, one of the best ways of improving your chances of success is to put up nest-boxes. To many, the bird nest-box is a recent invention, and most think simply in terms of the Blue Tit box in their back garden. However, the nest-box, and artificial nest sites in general, have had a long and chequered history.

THE HISTORY OF THE NEST-BOX

The idea of providing artificial nest sites for birds dates back nearly 2000 years, although the roots of the idea lie not in providing nest-sites for wild birds but rather in the factory farming of pigeons and doves for commercial gain. As early as 28 BC there are records of towers specially constructed for pigeons. These *columbaria* were entirely closed to the outside world, and the birds were kept in row upon row of holes (the origin of the word pigeonhole). They were apparently fattened up with bread (which had previously been chewed by a special group of slaves), and then slaughtered for the table. The birds were made more amenable by clipping their wings and breaking their legs, ensuring they could not fly, or even hobble, away.

From these rather barbaric origins developed the tradition of keeping Feral Pigeons in dovecotes on estates in the Norman times. Because of the Feral Pigeon's extended breeding season, fresh meat, in the form of adults and well-grown chicks (or squabs), was available through the autumn and early winter. This was very valuable, as other forms of meat were in short supply at these times. One inevitable by-product of pigeon farming was the vast quantity of droppings produced each year. This was not put to waste, but used as fertiliser on the surrounding agricultural land, and was particularly beneficial in the wine-growing regions of France.

As a result of agricultural improvements in the eighteenth century, other forms of meat became available throughout the year. The commercial value of pigeon farming decreased, and dovecotes became more ornamental than functional. However, many impressive examples still remain, and a particularly fine one, dating from the thirteenth century, is to be found at Westington Manor in Chipping Campden. This dovecote has about 1000 individual nest-boxes lining its walls. It was difficult to reach some of the higher boxes, so to overcome this problem a central vertical pillar, to which a ladder was attached, was built from the ground to the ceiling. This pillar could rotate, so that by standing on the ladder the farmer could push himself around the inside walls of the cote, and gain access to even the most remote of nest-boxes.

From these nest-boxes for pigeons were derived the first nest-boxes for wild birds, mainly for aesthetic reasons rather than commercial gain. Whilst there are records of nest-boxes in the form of clay flasks dating from the Middle Ages in the Netherlands, the first large-scale attempt at nest-boxing was carried out by Baron von Berlepsch in Germany at the turn of the century. Von Berlepsch attempted to attract insectivorous birds to nest on his estate in order to rid the area of a number of insect pests. He had no designs on which to base his nest-boxes, so he attempted to mimic nature as faithfully as he could. When designing a box for Woodpeckers, for example, he actually cut down an old Woodpecker hole, split open the wood and carefully measured the interior dimensions of the hole and its entrance. He was then able to base his nest-box design on these measurements. Such precision is not really necessary as the majority of hole-nesters are not as fussy as this – indeed, because of the scarcity of nest-holes they cannot afford to be. In all, von Berlepsch put up 2000 boxes, ninety per cent of which were occupied by fourteen separate species of birds. Whilst the success of his nest-box programme cannot be doubted, whether or not this had any effect on the local insect populations is not recorded.

From these humble origins has sprung the enormous variety of nest-box designs that we have today.

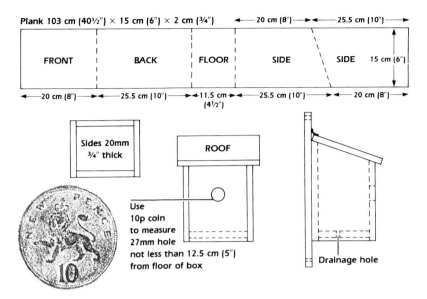

Plank 103 cm (40½") × 15 cm (6") × 2 cm (¾")

FRONT · BACK · FLOOR · SIDE · SIDE   15 cm (6")

20 cm (8") · 25.5 cm (10") · 11.5 cm (4½") · 25.5 cm (10") · 20 cm (8")

20 cm (8") · 25.5 cm (10")

Sides 20mm ¾" thick

ROOF

Use 10p coin to measure 27mm hole not less than 12.5 cm (5") from floor of box

Drainage hole

THE BASIC NEST-BOX

The basic nest-box is simplicity itself: a box with an entrance hole and a hinged sloping roof, to ensure water run-off and to allow inspection.

In general, wood is the most suitable material from which to construct a box. Given the cost of wood, it is well worth bearing in mind that the actual dimensions of the box are not critical, and it is best to design the box to fit the available wood rather than the other way around. A number of other materials are used, although less extensively, in the construction of nest-boxes. Metal and plastic boxes tend to suffer from condensation and may cause the brood to overheat in hot weather; and concrete boxes, although very durable, are difficult to manufacture and heavy to put up. However, one great advantage of concrete boxes is their resistance to the unwanted visitations of squirrels and Woodpeckers. In some areas where boxes have been used extensively, the local Great Spotted Woodpeckers have learnt to associate boxes with an easy meal; by boring through the front of the nest-box, they can gain access to the nest chamber, thus successfully destroying the box as well as the brood.

A simple hinge, made from leather or a strip of rubber from the inner tube of a tyre, is ideal for attaching the roof to the box. Avoid using metal hinges, as these will rust in time. It may be tempting to fit a small perch onto the front of the box, but this is not to be recommended. The parents will rarely use it, yet it may enable potential predators to gain access to the nest more easily.

Whilst it is rarely possible to be certain which species will take over any particular box, you can control this to a certain extent by varying the diameter of the entrance hole. For example 3.2cm is perfect for Pied Flycatchers and Redstarts, but if House Sparrows become a nuisance, this could be reduced to 2.9cm to exclude the unwanted guests.

Finally, if you are keen to atttract a summer visitor to breed in one of your boxes, it is a good idea to block the entrance hole until the species has arrived from its wintering grounds. Although this does not always work, it at least increases the chances that you will attract the correct species.

PUTTING UP NEST-BOXES

To achieve success with your nest-box, a little forethought is necessary; in particular where do you put it, how do you attach it, at what height and, if you are putting up more than one box, how many boxes should you put up in a given area?

The majority of boxes are fixed to trees. This is not only more pleasing to the eye, but any bird looking for a nest-hole is more likely to come across a box in this position; after all most nest-holes are in trees. Before fixing the box, make a note of the prevailing wind direction, and position it so that, in torrential rain, water does not pour into the nest cavity.

To fasten the box to the tree, it is often best to attach a vertical strip of wood to the back of the box. This batten should be longer than the rear depth of the box, so that the tongues of wood which protrude above and below the box can be used to fix the box to the tree. Never use steel nails or screws as these will rust rapidly and cannot be adjusted – which may be necessary if the tree is still growing. Instead, use galvanised screws and nails. Check the fastenings of the box at the beginning of each season, as occasionally a growing tree may force nails out. If the box were to fall during nesting, the brood would be lost.

The box should be positioned high enough to be out of reach of predators, but not so high that it cannot be reached with a ladder. If you are thinking of putting up more than one box, it is important to realise that many species are territorial, and two neighbouring pairs will not tolerate nesting close together. For most species, five to ten boxes per hectare is suitable, although for colonial species (for example, Jackdaws, House Sparrows and House Martins) a number can be placed fairly close together.

VARIATIONS ON A THEME:
TYPES OF NEST-BOX

There is no space here to give detailed plans of all the various types of nest-box. Readers who wish to know more about specific designs for a variety of species are referred to the excellent British Trust for Ornithology publication *Nestboxes* by Chris du Feu.

Variations on the basic plan do exist, however. Instead of a simple entrance hole in the front of the box, some species prefer open-fronted boxes, in which the upper part of the box front is cut away. This type of box is particularly suitable for Spotted Flycatchers and Pied Wagtails, although the lucky nest-boxer may even attract a Kestrel. Because of its open front, these boxes should be placed carefully so that they are well out of the reach of predators.

Other types of box are more specialised in their use. The chimney box, originally designed for Tawny Owls, is a long thin box, square or rectangular in cross section, which is mounted at an angle of 45° to the horizontal, often on the underside of a branch. If the box is intended for owls, dry peat or wood chippings should be placed in the bottom, as owls will not line the nest themselves.

Species such as Kingfishers and Sand Martins which nest in holes in banks can be persuaded to nest in short lengths of plastic drainpipes sunk into river-banks. Indeed it is even possible to go one stage further and construct a bank in the first place.

The final type of box is perhaps the most specialised, but one of the most useful – the House Martin box. These are shaped rather like a quarter of a hollow sphere with a small entrance hole, and can be made from papier-mâché or bought commercially (as can most nest-boxes). By placing a number of these together under the eaves of your house, you may be able to initiate a breeding colony. One word of caution, though: nestling House Martins tend to be rather messy, and their droppings may prove a nuisance.

TYPES OF NEST-BOX

RIGHT TOP *Sand Martin nest-box*
The vertical shaft is lined with boxing. Length of horizontal access passage is not critical. Nest chamber is closed with a removable lid. Remember that Sand Martins nest colonially!

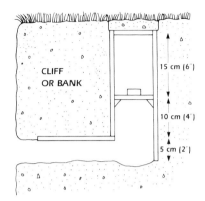

CLIFF
OR BANK

15 cm (6″)

10 cm (4″)

5 cm (2″)

RIGHT *'Chimney' nest-box*
For Tawny Owls. Perforate the base for drainage and prime the nest place with a layer of peat or sawdust. Put the box under a lateral tree branch at an angle of about 30° from the vertical.

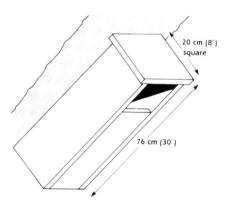

20 cm (8″) square

76 cm (30″)

BELOW *House Martin box*
Put up a row of them, but they are most successful when martins are already nesting nearby.

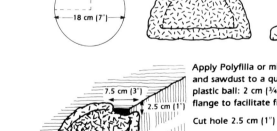

18 cm (7″)

Flange

7.5 cm (3″)

2.5 cm (1″)

Apply Polyfilla or mixture of cement and sawdust to a quarter segment of plastic ball: 2 cm (¾″) thick, leaving flange to facilitate fixing to wall.

Cut hole 2.5 cm (1″) deep and 7.5 cm (3″) wide

Mount on board and fasten to wall or fix directly to wall with mixture.

ARTIFICIAL NEST-SITES AND BIRD POPULATIONS

The humble tit box in the back garden is not only pleasing, it is also extremely valuable to the local tit population. The total area of gardens in the British Isles is nearly 300 000 hectares (almost twice the total area of national nature reserves), so they are clearly a very important habitat for birds. Over the last forty years, some fifteen per cent of Britain's deciduous woodland has been felled, and more than twenty per cent of its hedgerow removed. Much of the deciduous woodland has been replaced by conifers, which have few natural nest-holes. The felling of vast numbers of stands of dead and diseased elm trees has yet further reduced the number of potential nest-sites. Because of these changes to the British countryside, gardens are becoming increasingly important oases for bird-life, and providing nest-boxes allows some species to expand into towns.

Two species that have benefited greatly from extensive nest-box programmes are the Goldeneye and the Pied Flycatcher. The Goldeneye, a hole-nesting duck, was extremely rare as a breeding bird in Britain, its main breeding area being the lakes and rivers of the forested taiga zone of North America and northern Eurasia. In principle there was little reason for this species' scarcity in Britain as, apart from the lack of nest sites, the wooded lochs of Scotland provided an ideal habitat. To overcome this problem, a large number of nest-boxes were placed in likely sites, and the ever-expanding, although by no means large, population of Scottish Goldeneyes now nest almost entirely in nest-boxes.

The other species whose range has recently expanded with the help of nest-boxes is the Pied Flycatcher which, over the last thirty years, has expanded from its strongholds in Wales and northern England up into Scotland. Its preferred habitat is the deciduous woodland of upland valleys, in particular the Welsh sessile oak-woods. Often the only reason for its absence from woodlands within its range is the lack of natural nest-holes – because of the species or age of tree stands. In one nature reserve in Carmarthenshire with large numbers of nest-boxes, the breeding density of Pied Flycatchers was 120 pairs per square kilometre – twice that of a similar woodland without boxes.

In the Camargue, the delta of the River Rhône in southern

France, the provisioning of artificial nest sites has been taken to the ultimate extreme. Researchers there have created entire breeding colonies of flamingoes and egrets from scratch. In the case of the flamingoes, an entire island was bulldozed into shape in a safe and remote part of a saline lagoon. Artificial nests were built and after a few years flamingoes moved in from a nearby island which was being rapidly eroded away by the combined effects of wind and wave. The colony now numbers up to 20 000 breeding pairs each year, making it the largest breeding colony of flamingoes in Europe. A proportion of the birds are ringed, and can be told from one another by a letter code on the ring. These codes can be read by telescope from a specially constructed tower next to the colony, allowing a detailed study of their breeding biology.

Cattle Egrets have been encouraged to adopt artificial treetop nest ledges in the Camargue, where a group of trees was grown on an island specially created for them. Occasionally Cattle Egrets visit southern England and maybe one day they will stay to breed.

The egret story is perhaps even more remarkable, as it necessitated not only constructing an island surrounded by a moat, but also growing the trees in which the egrets would nest. Suitably fast-growing species of trees were planted, yet it still took nearly ten years before they were of a sufficient height to be used as nesting trees. The egrets were attracted with the help of decoys, food and ready-built nests, and within a few years the island became a thriving mixed species colony of Little Egrets, Cattle Egrets (attracted to the area for the first time) and Night Herons. The whole project was considered so successful that it is presently being repeated at a neighbouring site, although it will be a few years before the new colony is occupied.

THE NEST RECORD SCHEME

Once you have found a nest, or your new nest-box has been occupied, your interest need not stop there. Anyone who finds a nest, be it in a box or a natural site, is encouraged to record the details and submit their findings to the British Trust for Ornithology's Nest Record Scheme. This scheme was begun in 1939 under the name of the 'Nestling and Fledgling Enquiry' and, as it reaches its half-century, will have received and processed nearly three-quarters of a million nest records. By completing 'Nest Record Cards', observers throughout Britain and Ireland gather information about the breeding biology of a wide variety of species. These data can be used to determine the seasonal, annual and regional variation in the breeding success of many species of bird. This information, which is computerised and therefore readily accessible, has been the source of data for numerous scientific papers, and provides the foundation of much of our understanding of nesting birds. This, in turn, enables us to make informed and worthwhile contributions to species conservation.

OBSERVER				SPECIES		YEAR 19	B.T.O.Ref.
NO. of EGGS or YOUNG at each visit.				Record here stage of building, if bird sitting; if eggs warm; age of young; ring nos. etc.	COUNTY	if this record is entered on ATLAS CARD put ✓ in box:	Office Use Only
DATE Day ¦ Month	G.M.T.	EGGS	YNG				D
					LOCALITY (place-name) Grid Ref		C
							H
					ALTITUDE above sea level ....ft.		
					HABITAT ¦ Delete those inapplicable:- RURAL/SUBURBAN/URBAN		F
					NEST SITE		
Further visits, notes on outcome, etc. — ON BACK					Height above ground or cliff-base ....ft.		

The BTO has filed three quarters of a million nest record cards.

PARTICIPATING IN THE NEST RECORD SCHEME

Taking part in the scheme could not be more easy. Simply write to the British Trust for Ornithology (address p. 168) and they will supply you with both the instructions and the cards on which all records must be submitted. For each nest that you find, various sorts of information are required. On the card there are spaces for you to fill in your name, the species, the year, the location, the county and the altitude. Beside this, there is room for you to fill in information about the nest. Nest records are most valuable when a number of visits are made to the same nest, although cards for a nest which was only visited once are still useful. The stage of the nesting cycle is recorded at every visit (for example the stage of nest building, the clutch size and the brood size), as is the date. A wide variety of information can be calculated from these cards: laying dates, the intervals between egg laying, clutch size, incubation period, hatching success, brood size, nestling mortality, fledging period and breeding success. Needless to say, not all cards will contain this information, but once enough cards are available, very significant analyses can be made. Two final spaces on the card enable you to give information about the habitat in which the nest was found, and details of the nest site itself. This will, for example, enable researchers to determine how a species' choice of nest site and habitat has varied over the years in response to changes in agricultural practice.

In a scientific paper in 1938, David Lack wrote that 'field observation of birds is essentially the domain of the amateur...' This is certainly true of the Nest Record Scheme.

59

3

ADVENTURE OR MISADVENTURE?

Peter Grant

Several species of birds, like the Osprey and Barn Owl, have successfully expanded their world range over thousands of years and are now found from Australia to North America, wherever suitable habitat exists. Others, like the House Sparrow and Starling, are equally cosmopolitan, but have been brought to new continents by human hand and have thrived and spread across vast new regions. These are the successful ones in the bird world, able to colonise and survive as long as their relatively simple habitat and food requirements are met.

At the other end of the scale are those species which are so isolated or specialised that they are confined to a single island, mountain range or forest, their very existence as fragile as the delicate ecosystem on which they depend.

The geographical distribution of the majority of the rest of the 8000 or 9000 species of birds in the world is constantly changing. The population of each species expands or contracts in response to climatic or environmental changes. Habitat destruction, changes in land-use and climatic disasters such as drought or flood are easily identified factors, but other changes can be so subtle that their effects on bird populations remain unexplained.

In the fight for survival, all species strive to keep their numbers as high as possible. Various strategies are employed to produce the maximum number of young. Perhaps the most remarkable of these is migration, used to get the most out of the available habitats and sources of food by moving with the seasons. The efficiency of the migration strategy must be excellent because, at the end of the day, each species must produce enough young to offset the periodic and sometimes great mortality suffered during dangerous, long-distance journeys.

During migration, some birds inevitably go astray, forced off route by adverse weather systems or pushed too far by an overstrong migratory urge. But are these waifs and strays really lost? Or is it perhaps more likely that this is yet another built-in strategy for survival and range expansion, enabling species to sample and possibly colonise new grounds?

COLONISATION

Whatever the truth, the wandering and vagrancy of birds adds a fascinating extra field of interest to the hobby of birdwatching. In this chapter, we look at examples of natural range expansions and contractions in Britain, and how several species have colonised and spread after having been first brought to the region by man. We also look at the rapidly growing and increasingly well-organised rare-bird scene, a new sport at the popular end of ornithology for which off-course migrants are the essential ingredient. The good thing is that the mass of data gathered by the 'just-for-pleasure' band of amateur birders and rare-bird enthusiasts eventually builds into new and important ornithological knowledge. It provides the basic nuts and bolts which enable the more scientific ornithological analyst to monitor and understand changes in distribution, the mysteries of migration and its changing patterns, and the knottier aspects of bird identification.

THE COLLARED DOVE

By far the most exciting and interesting form of colonisation is that which occurs naturally, as opposed to colonisation following introduction by man or escapes from captivity. Sometimes, as in the case of the Collared Dove, the colonisation process can be remarkably swift. This species formerly occurred in southwest Asia, but at the

Collared Doves. From twitcher's dream to a common bird in ten years!

end of the last century began a slow spread northwestwards through Europe. Later, the expansion accelerated, covering a spectacular 1000 miles of territory from the Balkans to the North Sea in just twenty years prior to 1948, the year it first nested in Denmark. The first Collared Dove recorded in Britain (in Lincolnshire in 1952) was initially thought to have escaped from captivity, but in the light of subsequent events it was almost certainly the original wild pioneer of Britain's most remarkable bird colonisation. In 1955 the Collared Dove was proved to nest here for the first time, at Cromer in Norfolk: no question of the bird having escaped from captivity this time. By 1963, just eight years later, the Collared Dove had been seen or had bred in every English county, and was further establishing itself in Wales, Scotland and Ireland. For the first few years of its colonisation, birdwatchers travelled to see the rarity as it spread to new localities, and in their fieldwork recorded the increase in numbers. Articles appeared in birdwatching magazines on how to tell it apart from the similar Barbary Dove or other doves kept by aviculturalists, and its spread was faithfully recorded in detail in each county bird report. Drawing on this information, Robert Hudson summarised the Collared Dove's colonisation of Britain and Ireland up to 1970 in two major papers in *British Birds* magazine, by which time an estimated breeding population of 15 000 to 25 000 pairs had been established. In just fifteen years, the Collared Dove had evolved from the latest rarity on the wanted list of every keen birder to a familiar bird of back gardens. Its increase continued, and in some areas it has even become an agricultural pest.

CETTI'S WARBLER

Several other colonists have established new breeding populations during the past few decades, but because they have rather specialised habitat requirements they have been held back from blanket colonisation like that of the Collared Dove. Cetti's Warbler, for example, is a bird of overgrown marsh-edges and waterways. Until about seventy years ago, it was confined to the Mediterranean region. After a gradual spread north through Europe, it was first seen in Britain in 1961, and was proved to breed here for the first time in 1973. By 1984, it had spread to over one hundred suitable localities mainly in southern England, with a total breeding population probably in excess of three hundred pairs and still steadily increasing. The tenacity of Cetti's Warbler has been surprising. After its initial colonisation, it was expected that the first severe winter would end or contain its attempts at permanent colonisation, but this proved not to be the case. Prolonged freezing conditions and heavy snow cover during February 1987 did, however, decimate the Cetti's Warblers at least in the Stour Valley area of Kent, which was where the species first nested in Britain in 1973 and which subsequently became its main stronghold. The full picture of how it has fared elsewhere in southern England has yet to emerge, but clearly its spread has suffered a major setback. Perhaps its status in Britain will become similar to that of our other non-migratory warbler species, the Dartford Warbler, whose population is periodically drastically reduced by severe weather, but which recovers during periods of milder winters. Whatever happens, its specialised habitat requirements will not allow it to become a common garden bird as was the case with the Collared Dove.

As is the case with any new colonist, the rarity value of Cetti's Warbler has ensured that the progress of its colonisation has been fully recorded by the amateur birdwatching network and by more scientifically orientated ornithologists working at some of the species' main colonies in southern Britain. This provides one of many examples whereby a species' rarity appeal prompts enthusiastic research and, in the case of Cetti's Warbler, many more facets of its biology are now better understood than would have been the case if it had never ventured from its former Meditterranean distribution.

THE BLACK REDSTART AND THE LITTLE RINGED PLOVER

The Black Redstart and the Little Ringed Plover are two other recent colonists which, like the Cetti's Warbler, require a rather special habitat in which to nest. One particularly interesting feature of their colonisation, however, is that whereas the Cetti's Warbler moved into habitat which has always existed in Britain, the Black Redstart and Little Ringed Plover adopted new habitat which had been inadvertently created by man.

The Black Redstart is a widespread breeding species on the European mainland. Its natural habitat is the rocky slopes and crags of mountain areas or sea cliffs. In its continental strongholds, it has also moved into urban areas, where buildings provide artificial crags and cliffs. Until the early 1940s, it nested only occasionally in Britain, in a few coastal areas which provided the correct nesting habitat. Then bombed areas in London and Dover provided a new artificial nesting habitat, and many pairs moved in and thrived. A viable breeding population was rapidly established in these areas, with the bombed sites in the very heart of the City of London as the major stronghold. As the bombed sites were redeveloped, the by then well-established population moved to other derelict areas and also took

Black Redstarts – rarities breeding in an industrial setting.

advantage of relatively undisturbed industrial complexes such as power stations, gas-works and disused railway sidings. Such sites remain the species' present-day stronghold in Britain, and around one hundred pairs breed annually.

The Little Ringed Plover took advantage of the gravelly bottom of a newly constructed, unfilled reservoir at Tring in Hertfordshire when it nested for the first time in 1938. The natural nesting habitat of the Little Ringed Plover is the gravelly margins or islands of wide rivers, and it was presumably a pair of over-zealous, 'lost' migrants, which had overshot their usual European breeding areas, which 'found' the newly-created habitat in England and thus established the species' foothold on new territory. More reservoirs, and an increase in gravel excavation which also creates suitable habitat for nesting Little Ringed Plovers, has led to a steady further expansion in Britain and a sharp increase in the number of breeding pairs. These delightful small waders now nest in many places throughout eastern and central England, and the total population is probably well over four hundred pairs.

FULMARS

It was the activity of man, rather than his creation of new habitat, that apparently led to one of the most spectacular range expansions of any British bird. If birdwatching had been a popular hobby in the middle of the last century, it would have been necessary to make a special expedition to the island of St Kilda, fifty miles west of the Outer Hebrides, to tick off a Fulmar on any life list. St Kilda had held the only British nesting colony of Fulmars for many centuries, but in the 1870s it began a remarkable population explosion. It is now a familiar bird seen off all coasts of Britain and Ireland, breeding wherever suitable cliff nesting-ledges and holes can be found. The amazingly rapid increase and spread is usually attributed in the main to the growth of the whaling and fishing industries, and especially to the practice of processing fish on factory ships at sea. This made large amounts of fish offal available for the first time, and enabled an ever larger population to be supported. The same factor is thought to be mainly responsible for the massive population growth and range expansion of the Kittiwake in Britain, although a decrease in the numbers of Kittiwakes being hunted by man for food was doubtless also a major factor in the case of this species.

It is difficult to believe, however, that such sudden and dramatic population explosions can always be so simply explained. Some scientists believe that some sudden genetic change must also have taken place in species like the Fulmar and Collared Dove to prompt a less sedentary, more migratory, existence. If this is the case, any environmental change should then be seen as merely a contributory, subsidiary factor.

HOOPOES

Some species, it seems, will never succeed in forming a viable breeding population in Britain, but not for the want of trying! Every spring, for example, the southern half of Britain receives its annual 'crop' of Hoopoes.

Between fifty and one hundred and fifty come every spring, and the sight of this pink bird, with its showy fan-like crest and black-and-white barred wings and tail, is regular enough on southern British lawns in April. Hoopoes are most numerous in periods of fine, warm weather when small numbers migrate far beyond their normal southern European range. But the British climate rarely lives up to such early-spring promise, with the result that Hoopoes manage to breed in Britain only once or twice every decade. The main diet of Hoopoes is grasshoppers, crickets and lizards, and Britain just does not have enough to sustain the Hoopoe on any regular basis. The showy colours of the Hoopoe – and its diet – are clearly better suited for its usual breeding range in the Mediterranean region, and not for the unreliable British summer. But long may the occasional sight of this exotic creature continue to bring a flutter of excitement to the hearts of Britain's birdwatchers.

BEE-EATERS

Much rarer in Britain, and even more colourful, the Bee-eater has also failed to establish a regular breeding population in northern Europe, simply because there are not enough bees and other large insects to support a breeding colony. Bee-eaters have nested in Britain on only a couple of occasions but, like the Hoopoe, a few pioneering vagrants continue to come each spring to explore British nesting possibilities.

In a similar category is the Black-winged Stilt, a pair of which nested for only the second time in Britain at Holme in Norfolk in 1987, amid a blaze of publicity. They were successful in raising young, and it is less easy to identify factors which prevent this species from nesting regularly in Britain than for the Hoopoe or Bee-eater.

OTHER RARE VISITORS

Several other species nest spasmodically in Britain without ever establishing a regular or expanding population. Despite plenty of apparently suitable habitat, birds such as the Mediterranean Gull, Savi's Warbler, Firecrest and Serin have bred for many years in very small numbers without ever making a breakthrough to more substantial colonisation. These species are simply on the outer limits of their range, and in most cases it is impossible to see which factors draw the boundary line. Breeding pairs of Firecrests in Britain vary each year from very few to 150 or more, and it is probable that the variation stems from weather patterns during their apparently rather random northward migration paths each spring: if easterly winds predominate, then more Firecrests are diverted across the English Channel and the North Sea, and the breeding population during the summer is proportionately higher.

While most of the colonists discussed so far have expanded from southern Europe, other species – like Temminck's Stint, Redwing, Fieldfare and Brambling – have begun to colonise Scotland from northern Europe.

DECLINING SPECIES

On the debit side, contractions of range have led to the loss or marked decline of certain species in Britain. The Wryneck and Red-backed Shrike, formerly widespread in southern England, have now all but disappeared; and the drastic decline of the Woodlark and Cirl Bunting in the same area continues apace. There is no ready explanation for these changes: habitat loss may have contributed to the decline in some areas, but the main factor is probably some subtle climatic or environmental change which has just tipped the scales against their ability to maintain a viable population.

Slight expansions and contractions at the edges of the geographical range of most species are happening all the time. Such adjustments are not life-threatening so long as the species continues to thrive in the heartlands of its range, but at the outer limits (southern England in the cases of Wryneck, Red-backed Shrike, Woodlark and Cirl Bunting) the effect is sorely felt. Alarming as the loss or decline of these species may appear to conservationists in Britain, there is probably little that can be done to influence this natural ebb and flow. Where man-created problems are not a factor, it is sensible to regard such changes as normal.

NEW NESTING SPECIES

It is heartening that the last several decades have shown more breeding species gained than lost. And the published records of rare-bird occurrences indicate that more species could shortly be nesting here for the first time. The Scarlet Rosefinch, spreading westwards across northern Europe for many years, has already nested once, in Scotland in 1982, after a steadily increasing number of vagrant arrivals across Britain from Scilly to Shetland. This trend of increase is continuing, and a regular breeding population will almost certainly be established soon. The Greenish Warbler, from the same region, is following in the footsteps of the Scarlet Rosefinch and, if vagrant records continue to increase at the present rate, is expected to breed here for the first time within a decade or two. Perhaps most remarkable of all, the massive increase in records of the Ring-billed Gull indicate that it could become the first North American species to colonise the Old World as a regular breeder. First recorded in Britain only as recently as 1973, nearly one hundred are now being seen each year along mainly western coasts. This dramatic change, arising from a combination of a massive population explosion in North America and a series of severely cold winters which forced longer-than-usual migrations, must inevitably lead to European colonisation in the near future. In fact, from the timing and pattern of its occurrence in Britain, many people believe that the Ring-billed Gull may already be nesting somewhere in northern Europe, perhaps as yet undetected among a colony of the similar-looking Common Gull, a species with which it often associates on its increasingly frequent visits to Britain.

ARTIFICIAL COLONISTS

Another group of colonists have a less instant appeal to the bird-watching purist. These are the rather mixed bag of species which have arrived not by any natural process of range expansion, but which have been either deliberately imported and released into suitable habitats, or have accidentally escaped from captivity and now breed in the wild. The guardians of the official British and Irish bird list, the British Ornithologists' Union (BOU), place these 'artificial' colonists apart from our native species in special Category C of the list. Category C is defined as 'species which, although originally introduced by man, have now established a regular feral breeding stock which apparently maintains itself without necessary recourse to further introductions'. While attempts have been made to introduce a large variety of exotic species, and they have occasionally bred successfully in the wild, only those which have maintained a viable and self-maintaining population for a period of many years are formally admitted to Category C by the BOU. Thus despite many attempts to introduce free-flying Budgerigars at various estates and wildlife parks in Britain, none has been successful, and the species has so far failed to gain a place on the official list. Such a colony thrived for many years on Tresco in the Isles of Scilly after their initial introduction in 1969, and grew in size to about one hundred pairs. When winter food ceased to be provided, however, the colony dwindled rapidly and none now remain.

It is perhaps surprising that only ten species from the innumerable introductions and escapes have succeeded in meeting the requirements for admission to Category C. Five of these – Canada Goose, Egyptian Goose, Mandarin Duck, Golden Pheasant and Lady Amherst's Pheasant – were initially imported and released for no other reason than to grace the lakes and woodland of private estates, giving an exotic touch to match the architectural splendour and magnificently furnished interior of the stately home. Many other species of colourful or elegant waterfowl and gamebirds have also been imported for this purpose (the Peacock is perhaps the best-known example) but none has been sufficiently suited to the British climate or environment to establish a self-maintained presence. Of these five species, four are still found only in isolated pockets of suitable habitat, requiring a special journey for the birdwatcher who wishes to add them to his list. Only the Canada Goose has managed to spread widely throughout Britain, and it is now a familiar sight on most large waters in England and Wales. In Britain, it is largely a resident species in most areas, but some populations here and especially in northern Europe have established lengthy migratory flight-lines like those still undertaken by the native population in North America.

Like the Canada Goose, two other Category C species have become such a familiar and widespread part of British ornithology that it is sometimes difficult to appreciate that they are not native to the region. The Pheasant, now well-established throughout Britain, was introduced from various parts of Asia (the most familiar white ring-necked form came from China), and the Red-legged Partridge, now widespread in England, was brought from southern Europe.

Both species were primarily introduced to provide additional quarry on hunting estates.

In view of its widespread presence across most of England and Wales, it is also surprising that the Little Owl has never been an indigenous British bird. It was introduced from Europe to several areas in England during the latter half of the last century.

The two most recent admissions to Category C, Ruddy Duck in 1971 and Ring-necked Parakeet in 1983, both developed self-maintaining populations from individuals which had escaped from captivity. The Ruddy Duck now numbers flocks of 400 to 500 on Midlands reservoirs in winter, and the breeding range is steadily expanding. About seventy free-winged juveniles of this attractive North American duck escaped from the Wildfowl Trust headquarters at Slimbridge in Gloucestershire between 1956 and 1963, and it is from this nucleus that the feral breeding population grew.

The Ring-necked Parakeet is perhaps the most exotic of all species to be added to the British and Irish list. Its bright colours and raucous flight-call are much more suited to tropical regions, but by starting the colonisation of Britain it is repeating similar colonisations in other temperate regions of the world. The Ring-necked Parakeet is a popular cage-bird, and a mass escape from a consignment imported from its native India or Africa is thought to be the main origin of the feral population. At present, it is mainly confined to the London suburbs and parks and to a few isolated parts of Kent, visiting bird tables and nesting in tree holes. The Ring-necked Parakeet has

A Ring-necked Parakeet – now in Category C of the British and Irish bird list.

become an agricultural and horticultural pest in grain- and fruit-growing areas, in other parts of the world, and there are fears that it may also become so in Britain in due course.

Although officially listed as Category A species (the category for indigenous British birds), three species owe their continued presence in the wild to introductions which bolstered or replaced dwindling or extinct British populations. The Capercaillie, Greylag Goose and Mute Swan were all re-introduced mainly for hunting interests.

Attemps to re-introduce the White-tailed Eagle in western Scotland have recently been successful, and young have been reared in the wild. This species has been extinct as a British breeder since 1916, and if a lasting population is established it will be the first example of a successful re-introduction that has been undertaken purely for conservationist reasons.

TWITCHING

Although artificial introductions and re-introductions of birds can bring a certain extra interest to the birdwatching scene, it is nowhere near as great as that brought by naturally occurring changes in bird distribution. Natural alterations of range depend largely on the vagaries of migration, causing pioneering individuals to venture beyond their normal range to sample new territory. Only a tiny fraction of these vagrant pioneers is ever successful, but each one potentially provides the spice of the unexpected rarity sighting which adds so much to the fascination of birdwatching.

The wandering and vagrancy of birds has also spawned a remarkably fast-growing and popular aspect of the modern birdwatching scene called 'twitching', in which birders travel to a specific locality to see for themselves the latest off-course rarity in order to collect it as a new tick on their life list. Twitching is a pursuit often scorned by some old-school ornithologists as a waste of time, unscientific and pointless, like collecting train numbers. To the outsider, it's a mysterious pastime, with its own jargon and obscure motivation. But to the ardent twitcher the appeal is obvious, with the chase providing a narcotic blend of excitement, challenge, competition and one-upmanship, as well as requiring a considerable amount of skill to identify the object of the hunt. In addition, there is the enjoyable social gathering of like-minded enthusiasts at each rare-bird venue – all the ingredients, in fact, of any other popular pastime.

Although it is true that deep scientific thought is often far from the mind of the avid twitcher, the information gathered and published as a result of the quest for rare birds can be of considerable value to the student of bird migration. It also provides direct evidence for the first pioneering movements of birds which occasionally lead to new colonisations and range expansions. This new form of birdwatching, too, has sharpened field identification know-how by developing a thirst for knowledge on how to tell the rarer species from a similar and commoner relative. Clearly, you must first be certain that the bird is, for example, a vagrant Red-necked Stint (from Asia) and not an on-course Little Stint (from Europe) before alerting the twitching hordes or adding it to your life list.

Whatever the scientific value of their pursuit, there can be no doubt that twitchers form by far the most fanatical and single-minded band in birdwatching. An overnight journey of several hundred miles is quite normal in order to arrive as soon as possible at the scene of the latest rarity. Twitchers are drawn from all age-groups and backgrounds, gathering shoulder-to-shoulder to marvel at the latest addition to their life lists. A prime attraction can bring a crowd of many hundreds to some remote rural spot.

In the 1970s, when mass twitching began to take off, such hordes brought problems, with reports of trampling feet causing habitat damage or, in one notorious case, a trespassing crowd being muck-sprayed by an irate farmer; but twitchers have now put their own house in order with a code of conduct, better communication, and proper organisation. Wardens once dreaded the arrival of a major rarity on their reserves, for fear of the inevitable twitcher invasion. Now, aware of the new organisation and responsible approach among the twitching hordes, however, they increasingly welcome such an event by making special arrangements to handle the surge of visitors. Not only is each new twitching recruit an ardent supporter of the reserve system and bird conservation in general, but they also willingly put hands in pockets to make contributions to the upkeep of the reserve – a happy outcome, which has built many a new hide or financed other management projects.

The previously informal twitcher grapevine, by which news was spread instantly by telephone calls among twitching friends, is now properly organised on a commercial basis: dial 0898 700222, and you will instantly be brought up-to-date with the latest national rare-bird information. For the big rarity, directions and map references are given, with details of any special access arrangements to reserves or private land. The taped message 'Birdline' is operated by the Bird Information Service, a new organisation founded in January 1987 which also publishes *Birding World* magazine (issued monthly and packed with birding news and information!)

Born of better roads, more leisure time and a wider general interest in wildlife, twitching now numbers several thousand regular 'long distance' *aficionados*. The numbers are swollen by many other less fanatical birdwatchers who are happy just to 'pop up the road' to see a rarity near their local patch. Of course, there's no guarantee that the bird will not have flown away by the time you get there, but that's all part of the challenge of twitching, and the cause of the euphoria felt when the bird is seen after a drive of several hundred miles!

Basic twitching equipment is a pair of binoculars (most twitchers now also carry a telescope and tripod), a field guide or two, a road map and a car.

Also essential, but not for sale in any shop, is a collector's fascination for rare and often beautiful creatures – the basic appeal of twitching and rare birds is much the same as that for rare stamps or rare books. It surprises old hands, who have gone through the bird-learning mill since schooldays, that even basic identification skills no longer seem important. Many new converts to twitching could not tell a female Reed Bunting from a female Yellowhammer, but they happily tick off a Little Bunting when it is pointed out.

OFF-COURSE IN SCILLY

A rare bird can turn up almost anywhere, but they occur with more regularity than anywhere else in the British Isles in October on the Isles of Scilly. Over two thousand twitchers join what has become the sport's event-of-the-year on the main island of St Mary's. The invasion is welcomed by the islanders as a valuable extension of their tourist season. The islands, off Britain's southwesternmost limb, are well outside Europe's main bird migration corridors, but their situation collects a guaranteed October harvest of off-course migrants from America, Asia and Africa.

Each morning, a binocular- and telescope-clad army of bird-watchers emerges from the hotels, guest houses and self-catering cottages to scour the island for any newly arrived rarities. Hopes are perhaps highest after a few days of strong westerly winds, the conditions most likely to bring a vagrant from North America. Normally, migrant birds from Canada are moving southwards to wintering areas in the southern USA or South America. Many fly non-stop due south from eastern Canada, a route which takes them out over the open western Atlantic, heading for Florida or South America. Some are caught out by fast-moving cyclonic weather systems which lift them high into westerly jet streams and deposit them 2500 miles off course at the first European landfall. On Scilly, with so many pairs of binoculars on the look-out, very few escape human gaze for long. Some, of course, fail to make the crossing and perish in the ocean. Others hitch a lift on ships and fly off when land comes into view.

Given certain weather conditions, birds can be whisked across the Atlantic well within their normal capacity for thirty to fifty hours of sustained flight. Usually only one or two individuals arrive, sometimes in exhausted condition. At other times, when weather conditions are just right, larger numbers come, like the eight Blackpoll Warblers, five Grey-cheeked Thrushes, three Rose-breasted Grosbeaks and two Nighthawks in October 1976, the flock of fifteen Buff-breasted Sandpipers on St Mary's golf course in September 1977, or the record seventeen North American species seen on Scilly during the autumn of 1983. The islands' bird list of 370 includes a total of no less than fifty American species, a number (and proportion) far in

excess of that of any other European locality.

Word of any new rarity find spreads like wildfire, bringing the birders hurrying to the spot. The great rarity finds on Scilly go down in twitcher folklore. An 800-strong crowd gathered along the battlement-like wall which surrounds the Garrison on St Mary's on 10 October 1983 to watch a Cliff Swallow hawking for insects in the lee of the wall. It put on a magnificent show for its gallery of admirers, often flying so close as to whistle past their ears. This bird was originally identified as a Red-rumped Swallow, a rare enough wanderer from southern Europe, but when more expert eyes arrived it was re-identified as a Cliff Swallow, normally a resident of North America but then making its first recorded journey to Europe.

When a rare bird is discoverd on one of the other islands, the birding crowds fill the tripper launches and, like an invading army, land on the nearest convenient beach. Special organisation is sometimes needed to control the crowds, like the ticket system hastily organised in October 1979 to let twenty birders at a time into a small private field to see a Blyth's Reed Warbler. By this method, over three hundred people saw the bird during a morning, demonstrating how well organised the twitchers can be when necessary. The fact that this bird subsequently proved to be a Marsh Warbler and not the very much rarer Blyth's Reed Warbler is the final twist in this tale.

In the evenings, the twitchers gather in the cellar of the Porthcressa Restaurant, home of tourist discos earlier in the season but in October venue for the nightly log-call of birds seen on the islands. This, too, is an important social event for the birders, giving them the chance to discuss everything from the latest piece of equipment to the finer points of some controversial rarity identification.

RARITY RECORDS

The massed gatherings in October on Scilly are the ultimate expression of the twitching and rare-bird scene, but the quest for rarities goes on throughout the year at every birdwatching hotspot from Fair Isle to Dungeness. Having found a rare bird, the next step is for the finders to get the record accepted and published by the ornithological Establishment. Official acceptance of any 'national' rarity (one which occurs on average ten or less times each year) involves a system of vetting set up in 1958 by the leading national bird magazine, *British Birds*. In that year, the British Birds Rarities Committee (BBRC) was established to bring order to the assessment and publication of the rapidly-growing number of observations of rarities. This had previously been done on a comparatively haphazard basis, with the editors of *British Birds* assessing the validity of each claim and piecemeal publication in the magazine's pages. The BBRC was the first national rare-bird vetting body to be established anywhere in the world, and its initiative and well tried and tested procedures have now been followed in most other countries where birdwatching is an established or growing activity.

The BBRC consists of its secretary and ten bird identification experts, one of whom retires each year to be replaced by a new member who is elected by the regional and county birdwatching societies. It deals with rare species occurring in England, Wales, Scotland and the Channel Islands. Records for the Republic of Ireland and Northern Ireland are dealt with separately by the Irish Rare Birds Committee. The BBRC's task has grown rapidly in recent years: it now considers over 1200 rarity claims each year, and has recently had to call on outside sponsorship to help with the cost of the operation.

To submit a claim, the observer sends full details and a description of the rarity to the BBRC secretary, preferably via the bird recorder of the county in which the sighting was made. Batches of claims are then circulated by post to BBRC members, each of whom then votes as to whether the claim should be accepted or rejected. For the record to be accepted and subsequently published, it must be supported by at least nine of the ten identification experts – a very stringent test which results in an average of two in ten submissions being rejected.

A rarity description should prove the identification and eliminate the possibility that a misidentification of some other similar species has occurred. If a distinctive rarity has been seen and described well, the acceptance procedure is almost a formality; but even a colourful and apparently unmistakable species such as a Roller or a Bee-eater is not infrequently rejected because the views or descriptions do not eliminate the possibility of confusion with another similar species.

The BBRC supplies its own Rarity Report Form on request, which makes it easier for records to be submitted and assessed. The form consists of a page on which all the basic details of the observation – observers' names, locality, weather, duration and distance of the observation and a full description of the bird – can be entered. For an easy-to-identify rarity, just a few lines of description is sufficient. The submission files for more difficult species, such as a tricky stint or warbler, include much lengthier documentation and a highly detailed, almost feather-by-feather description, often from several observers.

One pair of eyes will rarely notice every detail on a rare bird, and it is therefore always advisable to seek corroboration from other observers. This is especially true for any difficult-to-identify species, or one which is difficult to describe convincingly. In such cases it is often essential that the observer knows how to describe the bird accurately, by understanding how the various feather tracts 'fit together ' (its plumage topography), or how to tell whether it is in adult, juvenile, or immature plumage or moulting from one plumage to another. Such skills will enable plumage marks to be accurately described in relation to the particular feather tracts on which they occur, and ensure that any comparisons are made against similar, more common species in the same plumage stage. For example, it may not be enough to state that some of the feathers on its upper parts have pale fringes: to clinch the identification it may be important to define whether it is, for example, the scapulars, greater coverts or tertials which are so marked.

Such attention to detail is essential if a competent description is to be produced, sufficient to convince at least nine out of ten BBRC members. Such skill at description-writing does not come without a lot of experience and practice, emphasising the need to call for corroboration from an expert when necessary.

Bird Topography

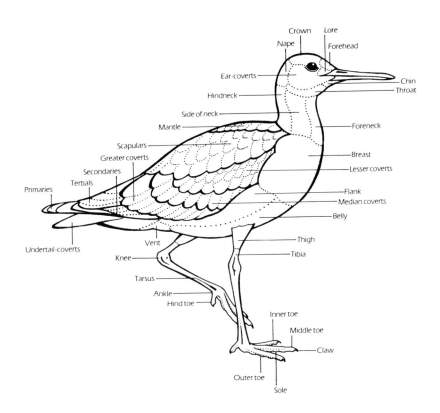

An increasing number of rarity claims are nowadays also supported by photographic evidence, taken by a growing band of highly skilled photographers who specialise in getting pictures of the major rarities. Good photographs obviously provide invaluable support for any rarity claim, and in several recent cases they have been the key to solving some especially controversial ones – notably a presumed Red-necked Stint on Fair Isle in 1982 (which was re-identified with the help of photographs as a Sanderling in worn adult summer plumage) and a claimed Western Sandpiper at Felixstowe, Suffolk, in 1982/83, now accepted as a Semipalmated Sandpiper. While the assessment of most records is straightforward, others may take several years and several recirculations of the committee.

The final product of all this deliberation appears each year in

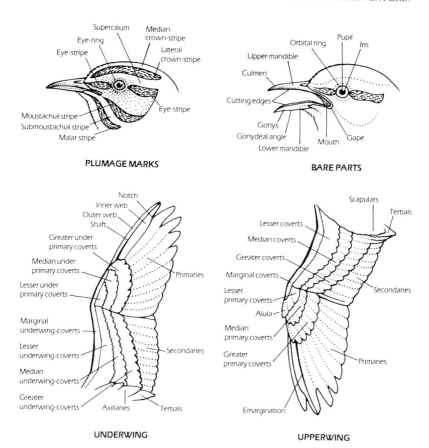

PLUMAGE MARKS

BARE PARTS

UNDERWING

UPPERWING

British Birds, which devotes most of its November issue to the 'Report on rare birds in Great Britain'. This 60-page report is the rare-bird hunters' yearbook, listing the details and observers for the more than 1000 officially accepted rarities recorded during the previous year. Illustrated with many photographs of the birds involved, it is the culmination of thousands of observer-hours in the field.

In addition to its listing in the report, any record of a species which has occurred five or less times in Great Britain is fully described and documented in a special article written by the observers – a valuable reference for readers keen to know what to look for should they ever come across the species themselves.

The dream of any rare-bird fanatic is to be the finder of the ultimate rarity – a species never seen before in Great Britain. An average of two or three new species is added to the official British and Irish List each year. These national 'firsts' are subjected to a further stage of assessment by the Establishment. Before a record can be added to the list, the record has to be passed not only by the BBRC, but also by the British Ornithologists' Union Records Committee (BOURC), a panel of ornithological veterans not noted for hasty decisions over new admissions. The process often takes several years, much to the frustration of birders keen for the official decision. Many amateurs, however, are largely unaware of the long-winded and painstaking international investigations involved, especially over the difficult question of whether the stray has arrived naturally or merely escaped from captivity. Once accepted, the full details of any national first are published as a paper in *British Birds*, written by the bird's finders.

Breeding records of rare birds in Great Britain are also carefully monitored and published by the Rare Breeding Birds Panel, run jointly by the RSPB and *British Birds*. The panel collates records gathered by the regional and county bird recorders and periodically publishes its report ('Rare breeding birds in the United Kingdom') in *British Birds* magazine. The data, in which locations are not divulged as a precaution against egg-collectors or disturbance by bird-watchers, provide a valuable permanent record of our threatened or colonising rare breeding species.

Pleasure birding and twitching now form a large and well-established part of the amateur network, making their own contributions to ornithological knowledge. Twitching is the ultimate expression of the 'pop' end of ornithology, combining the thrill of the chase and the 'collection' of rare and often beautiful birds on a life list. The ornithological value of rare-bird records may be far from the minds of the birdwatchers who seek them, but their observations often provide the first clues of important distributional changes. The mass of information is distilled into papers and books, and advances in field identification filter their way through the system to appear in each new field guide to the benefit of each new generation of birding enthusiasts. Birdwatching's main popular appeal is the unexpected observation of some rare or unusual species: one never knows what will happen next. Wherever it does happen, however, it is unlikely to be missed by the sharply tuned eyes of the ever-growing band of birders and twitchers.

4

THE NUMBERS GAME

Mike Moser and Robert Prŷs-Jones

A cold, clear evening on an estuary, with the watery sun sinking in the sky and the tide creeping in. A great flock of waders, Knot or Dunlin, erupts from its sandflat roost, then twists and wheels, with patterned precision, before subsiding back into tightly packed stillness a little further down the shore. It is spectacular sights like this which provide the stimulus for some of us to become hooked on birds. For others, it is simpler, more everyday encounters that arouse interest, like the Robin following us around the garden, searching for food in places where we have disturbed the earth.

TOGETHER OR ALONE

Interest breeds enquiry. Why do Knot occur together in huge numbers, whereas the Robin seems to lead an aggressively solitary life, chasing other Robins from its chosen acre of ground? Certainly it's not just a question of numbers. Knot are common enough in their estuarine habitats, with perhaps 250 000 visiting our shores each winter from their high Arctic breeding grounds; but Robins, in their millions, rank as one of Britain's commonest birds. Whether birds flock or lead a solitary life style depends on the differing ecological circumstances to which they are exposed.

We can gain more insights into this by considering species whose sociability alters as times change. To the casual observer, the

Wren is a solitary bird in summer or winter, flitting through the undergrowth and feeding on tiny invertebrates. Take a torch on a chill winter's night, however, and search the pitted stonework of the bridges over a nearby stream; it is highly likely that you will see a multitude of little eyes staring out from a hole. Eight, ten or more Wrens can be huddled in a tight little fluffed-up ball. Tiny, warm-blooded creatures like Wrens lose heat fast in cold weather as, in comparison with larger birds, their surface area is disproportionately large in relation to their body volume. Roosting in a sheltered hole, out of the wind, helps slow down heat loss, but making one chunky ball out of eight or more tiny bodies can help save much more again on a freezing night. Indeed, when Wrens choose to roost in a garden nest-box there may be several dozen of them huddled together.

More complex to understand fully is the much commoner situation of numerous individuals of a species flocking or roosting together. Many finches, buntings and other birds breed spaced out in pairs but feed and roost together outside the breeding season in flocks of tens, hundreds or thousands. Starlings feed in autumn or winter in flocks of a few dozen or more birds, but as evening draws on these small flocks progressively join together as the birds move toward their roost sites, until eventually many thousands flood into the patch of reeds or stand of trees where they will spend the night. Although these sites are invariably well-sheltered places, the birds do not huddle closely together and there is little evidence to suggest that heat conservation is an important consideration. Instead, escape from predators and more efficient gathering of food appear to be the key factors underlying this behaviour.

SAFETY IN NUMBERS?

There is mounting evidence that, for a bird which feeds in exposed situations, out on mudflats or in open fields, joining a flock may be a safety device, decreasing its chances of being captured by a predator. Thus, Woodpigeons in flocks detect attacking hawks at greater average distances than do solitary birds, giving them more time to escape, and, at least among small groups of birds, this benefit rises as flock size increases.

Other research has shown that birds in flocks can also spend more time feeding: the presence of many individuals together means that each need devote less time to looking around for predators. In flight, there may be further benefits from the 'confusion' effect, whereby a bird of prey finds it difficult, if not dangerous, to follow a potential victim amidst a swirling mass of other individuals.

Birds which group together in breeding colonies, such as many seabirds, may gain yet other advantages. In some cases the birds may combine to drive off predators; in others, the sheer numbers of eggs and young present may effectively 'swamp' the local predators with far more food than they need, ensuring that only a relatively small proportion are lost.

The advantages of flocking as a means of protection against attack are easy to envisage, if not always straightforward to demonstrate conclusively. Equally, however, there may be counterbalancing costs. A flock is more conspicuous than an isolated individual, and a flock's ability to detect predators more quickly would be of little advantage if the frequency of attack were greatly increased. In addition, it is difficult to see how improved avoidance of predators could solely be responsible for, say, the gathering together of numerous Starling flocks into massive nighttime winter roosts. This brings us to the concept of increased efficiency in obtaining food.

THE FOOD CONNECTION

The influence of food resources on the sociality of birds has been well demonstrated by studies on wagtails in spring. The birds were found to switch from flock feeding in the morning to solitary feeding in the middle of the day and then back to flock feeding in the evening. These changes tied in with the type of prey eaten. In the mornings and evenings, the birds congregated together to consume tiny midges, present in huge swarms in wet areas. In between, they searched cowpats for large dungflies, a more profitable prey than midges, but one which is only available during the warmer, middle parts of the day. Unlike the swarming midges, dungflies hide when disturbed and the wagtails therefore had to space themselves out widely, each defending a temporary territory around the area where it was foraging.

Terrestrial flocking birds like sparrows and buntings typically depend in autumn and winter on seeds and other vegetable foods which are distributed in patchy local concentrations. Individuals searching for food see others of their species already feeding and join them. Importantly, these patches of food are not fixed. A particular source may be depleted as increasing numbers of birds consume it, or may suddenly be made unavailable due to a covering of snow. Elsewhere, the ripening of seeds, their shedding from plants, or the activities of the farmer make new patches of food available. Small birds cannot survive long without feeding, and there must be strong selection on them to adopt behaviour which reduces the risk of failure to find food. This has been demonstrated by comparative studies on the energy reserves that different species carry to roost in winter. Bullfinches, living singly or in small groups and feeding on seeds from trees and bushes, whose distribution is predictable from one day to the next, have much lower fat reserves than similar-sized flocking species such as Reed Buntings and Yellowhammers, which depend on fallen grass and weed seeds taken from the ground. A Bullfinch needs merely to carry enough energy to survive the night, whereas the buntings must further insure against the risk of delay in finding food on the following day.

An important way of reducing risk is the exchange of information between individuals. A bird which locates food through noticing a flock of birds feeding at a particular site is making use of information that the presence of the flock provides as to the existence of suitable food there. Similarly, a bird already within a flock may learn by watching its neighbours how best to exploit the food that is present. At a less obvious level, by gathering together at night in large roosts, birds can make use of cues provided by other individuals as to where food is likely to be available on the following day. For example, birds which have done badly on one day might hold back in the morning and follow others whose confident direct flight indicates they may know where food is available. Complex laboratory and field experiments are beginning to reveal the reality of such information transfer between birds, and the process seems likely to be important in promoting gregariousness among many otherwise very different types of birds. Sand Martins or seabirds nesting colonially in summer might appear to resemble buntings or Starlings roosting colonially in winter in few ways, but all depend on unpredictable food sources. Swarms of insects, shoals of fish and clumps of fallen seeds all have scattered distributions which tend to vary from hour to hour and day to day.

POPULATION TRENDS

In some years, at least, Wrens may be the commonest birds in Britain, with a population possibly reaching ten million pairs, although in other years they are certainly less abundant, since the species is prone to sudden crashes in numbers. At the opposite end of the scale, the Purple Sandpiper was first recorded as a British breeding species only a few years ago, and there are still no more than a pair or two in Scotland. Such statistics raise a number of important questions: what are the factors that influence bird numbers? Why do we need to know? And, most importantly, how do we find out about them?

Weather is certainly an important factor and this is well demonstrated by the results of the BTO's national census of heronries, which has been carried out annually since 1928. Counts of breeding Herons at a proportion of their colonies have made it possible to track the fortunes of this species continuously for sixty years. The results are striking: although the numbers of Herons have varied tremendously over short-term periods, the population has remained relatively stable over the period as a whole. Analysis of these short-term declines and recoveries in relation to climatic conditions shows that the declines are brought about by severe winter weather, which restricts the birds' access to their food resources, whereas the recoveries occur during milder years. A similar susceptibility to severe weather is responsible for the periodic crashes in numbers of Wrens and several other species, and has shed light on which habitats are of key importance to different species. Thus, after a population crash, surviving Wrens breed in woodland or streamside vegetation the following year, only spreading back to gardens and finally hedgerows as their population rises again in subsequent years.

Fluctuations in the numbers of British birds need not necessarily be caused by changes in conditions within Britain itself. A classic example is that of a migrant warbler, the Common Whitethroat, which suffered a major population crash beginning in 1969. The species is only now beginning to recover. Similar, though less dramatic declines in a number of other migrant species pointed to the cause being severe drought in the Sahel region of north-central Africa, where all the affected species wintered. The drought meant that there was less food available for the birds and this restricted the populations that the Sahel was able to support; thus, despite continued breeding success in Europe, fewer birds could survive until the spring.

Short- or longer-term changes in the availability of food, often caused by changes in climatic conditions, are perhaps the most common natural influence on bird numbers. These climatic changes may be so slight that we find them difficult to recognise. For example

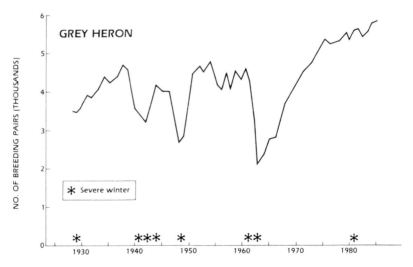

Annual fluctuations in numbers of nests of Grey Heron in England and Wales, from BTO Census of Heronries. Note the population crashes after severe winters and the relatively stable levels in interim years.

The Red-backed Shrike has almost disappeared in Britain.

the Red-backed Shrike, which was relatively common over much of southern England in the 1930s, now numbers at best only a few pairs. This decline probably stems from the slightly cooler, wetter spring weather in recent years which reduced the abundance of its large insect prey. Blackcaps, abundant as a breeding species but formerly rarely encountered in winter, appear to have benefitted from the recent upsurge in food available on bird tables and now overwinter in Britain in moderate numbers.

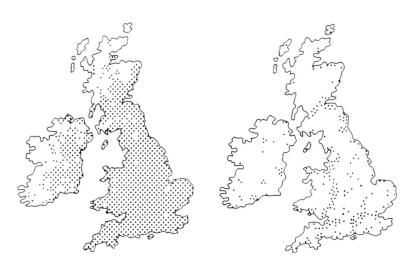

Breeding (left) and winter (right) distributions of the Blackcap.
The species overwinters more commonly than formerly, apparently
as a result of increased bird-table feeding.

Equally, however, one cannot turn to climate and food avail-ability to explain everything. The spectacular and rapid spread of the Collared Dove across Europe during the first half of this century sug-gests a genetic change within the species itself, enabling it to tolerate a more severe climate. Even more unexpectedly, periodic changes in the numbers of juvenile Dark-bellied Brent Geese wintering in Bri-tain, as well as in various wader species wintering in Africa, have been shown to be directly related to the numbers of lemmings on the Siberian tundra, where all these species breed! A fall in the numbers of lemmings causes their predators, such as Arctic foxes, to switch their attention to birds' nests, killing large numbers of young birds. A British bird census can thus indirectly supply information on a Siberian mammal population!

In today's world of massive technological development and human influence on the environment, man-induced changes in bird numbers are becoming not only more frequent but also more difficult to detect. It is easy to see how high levels of persecution reduced bird of prey populations during the last century, and how wetland recla-mation damaged marshland bird populations. Species such as the Osprey and Bittern declined to extinction in Britain, only to recolon-ise later this century in response to greater protection and careful habitat management. In the absence of total extinction, however, declines in populations of even large and conspicuous species may go undetected without careful censusing. This was compellingly demonstrated in the early 1960s, when the BTO undertook a census of the Peregrine Falcon – not because of worries over a decline in the species but through interest generated from a reputed increase in its numbers. This showed beyond doubt that the Peregrine Falcon population had fallen to unprecedentedly low levels. Investigation revealed that agricultural pesticide residues had been largely respon-sible, and this played a major role in alerting the British public to the problems inherent in their use.

More recently, censuses of Mute Swan populations have re-vealed the problems caused by lead pollution in freshwater environ-ments, and resulted in the phasing-out of lead weights by anglers and lead shot in gun cartridges.

An indirect consequence of the discovery of the effects of pesti-cides on Peregrines and many other wild birds was financial sup-port, from the Nature Conservancy Council, for the monitoring of farmland bird populations by means of the BTO's Common Birds Census. Results from this survey are continually throwing light on the ways in which changes in agricultural practice can affect wild bird populations. Thus, sustained declines in the numbers of some finches and buntings, such as the Linnet and Reed Bunting which depend on weed seeds for all or part of the year, are closely linked to the increased use of more efficient herbicides. A graph of the abundance of Reed Buntings over the past twenty-five years illustrates well both the short-term effects that cold winters have on this species and the longer-term influence of farmland management.

BIRD COUNTS

Bird populations are thus in a state of continuous flux, in response to both natural and man-induced environmental pressures. Some go up, some come down; some fluctuate widely, whereas others are relatively stable for extended periods. So, where does all the information come from that allows us to monitor these patterns? The answer lies with the army of amateurs who have turned their initial interest in birdwatching, possibly Britain's second largest participation hobby, into purposeful bird monitoring, thereby both increasing their own enjoyment and contributing to improved knowledge of our country's birdlife. By comparison with many other animals, birds are relatively easy to census, being large, often conspicuous and easy to identify even from a distance. But to provide a useful overall picture, the way in which such information is collected has to be standardised, and this requires the co-operation of people willing and able to synthesise the results. This, at a national level, is where the BTO comes in, co-ordinating fieldwork through an array of local bird clubs and regional representatives.

ATLASES, AND HOW YOU CAN HELP

Probably the most popular and best-known bird surveys are the bird atlases. 'Atlasing' is the mapping of the distribution of all the bird species in a given area – usually a county or a whole country. The first national bird atlas ever to be undertaken was carried out between 1968 and 1972 in Britain and Ireland by more than 10 000 bird-watchers from the BTO and the Irish Wildbird Conservancy. It was, at the time, the largest co-operative survey carried out by naturalists anywhere in the world! The project aimed to map the distribution of every breeding bird species in Britain and Ireland. The results were published in 1976 in *The Atlas of Breeding Birds of Britain and Ireland*, which has since become one of the most widely quoted ornithological publications in Britain. Following this, a winter bird atlas was successfully completed with enormous support from British birdwatchers, resulting in the publication of *The Atlas of Wintering Birds of Britain and Ireland* in 1986.

The great value of the atlas projects is that they provide a summary of bird distribution which can be used as a basis from which to monitor subsequent changes in the distribution and abundance of each species. To this end, fieldwork is beginning in the 1988 breeding season to update the first breeding bird atlas. This project has been sponsored by the Central Electricity Generating Board, and will involve fieldwork over three breeding seasons, with publication of the atlas in 1991. The fun part of atlasing is that any birdwatcher can contribute records from anywhere in Britain or Ireland: in fact, your holiday records if you are visiting the remoter parts of Britain and Ireland, where coverage is likely to be much harder to guarantee, will be particularly valuable. The results of this second breeding atlas will be awaited with some trepidation to see the extent of losses of species like lowland breeding waders, which have apparently suffered greatly as a result of agricultural intensification. If you would like to take part, please contact the BTO (address page 168).

Aside from the national atlases, many county bird clubs have completed their own local atlases. There is even a project under way right now to complete a European breeding bird atlas – the grandfather of them all! Finally, fieldwork for a very special sort of atlas is at present being carried out by the Nature Conservancy Council, studying the distribution of seabirds at sea around the British Isles. The survey is being conducted principally from ships, allowing bird densities in different sea areas to be mapped.

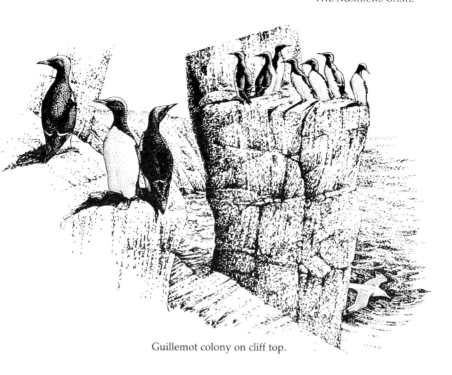

Guillemot colony on cliff top.

COUNTS OF COLONIAL BIRDS

Breeding colonies offer excellent opportunities for monitoring bird numbers, because the entire population of an area will be gathered together where they can be counted relatively easily. Disturbance should always be kept to an absolute minimum at nesting colonies and observations should be made from a distance, if possible. Always check with the local NCC or RSPB office or your BTO Regional Representative before making your first visit to a colony, as many are specially protected and are already being counted.

When counting colonial species, the first task is to find all the colonies in your area. Colonies usually occur on places such as islands, cliffs or in tall trees, which are inaccessible to predators. Once a site has been successfully occupied, it may be used for many years in succession. The famous heronry at Regent's Park, and the gannetries of Grassholm, Bass Rock, Noss and St Kilda, are well-known examples of such traditional sites; but even less conspicuous birds such as House Martins and terns will often use the same site year after year. For the birdwatcher, such traditions make monitoring much easier although there is always the danger of overlooking new colonies! These can best be found by checking all the sites which have suitable habitat; if occupied, the adult birds will quickly attract attention by their activity, particularly once there are young in the nest. Many seabird colonies can even be detected just by the noise and smell wafting up from the cliffs! If you are convinced that there is a colony (or roost) of Rooks, Herons, gulls or some other species in your area which you have failed to locate, one good way of tying it down would be to plot the flight lines of the adults on a map as they go out to feed and, with a bit of luck, the converging lines will lead you to the colony.

Counting large colonies of gulls, terns or cliff-nesting seabirds can be a real problem! Even after selecting the best time of year and finding a good viewing point, the sheer number of birds and frenzied activity are enough to mesmerise the inexperienced counter. Added to this, the presence of many non-breeding birds means that a count of all the adult birds would give a very inaccurate estimate of

Kittiwakes follow the fishermen.

the number of nesting pairs. The usual technique is therefore to count the apparently occupied nests, which can usually be distinguished from unoccupied nests by the copious white droppings which cover the side of the nest as soon as there are chicks. Hole-nesting species, such as the Sand Martin and the non-colonial Kingfisher, also leave plenty of evidence in this way to tell you which nest-sites are occupied. When counting very large colonies it is a good idea to divide them into sections, keeping accurate sub-totals of the nests in each area. Photography can be very helpful, particularly for large, white species such as Kittiwakes, and by piecing together a series of good black and white prints of the colony, the nests can be counted at leisure in the comfort of your home. Aerial photography can be useful in some special circumstances, such as the censusing of island-top gannetries which may number tens of thousands of pairs.

WADER AND WILDFOWL COUNTS

The estuarine waders form large roosts when their feeding areas are covered at high tide. Estuaries are a particularly threatened habitat and naturalists have observed the waders' roosting behaviour for many years to obtain counts of populations and evaluate sites. The Birds of Estuaries Enquiry, Britain's national programme for monitoring estuary birds, is organised by the BTO, with support from the NCC and RSPB. The project relies on co-ordinated teams of observers visiting the roosts on every estuary on a selected date once each month. The count dates coincide with high spring tides, when all the feeding areas are covered. Counting waders in winter can be a cold, wet and yet immensely rewarding pastime. Several tens of thousands of waders tightly packed together on a single roost make a splendid spectacle. Species such as Oystercatchers and Curlews cease feeding well before high tide and form small sub-roosts, which are often much easier to count than when the birds are massed together at high tide. Others, such as Knots, Bar-tailed Godwits and Dunlins, often arrive at the high tide roost in an enormous mixed-species and swirling flock. Here the only opportunity to make a count is probably after high tide, when the birds begin to disperse away from the roost, spreading out along the tideline.

Wildfowl are also counted during the winter months in Britain for the National Wildfowl Counts, a programme which has been organised by the Wildfowl Trust since 1947. The counts now cover more than 1000 sites in Britain, on a monthly basis from September to March. In general, the wildfowl are much easier to count than the waders because their larger size and more dispersed flocks allow quite accurate counts to be made simply by scanning with a telescope. The long run of counts has revealed that, perhaps surprisingly, many species of wildfowl have actually increased in Britain over the last thirty years, due to a decrease in hunting and the creation of artificial expanses of water.

ROOST COUNTS

In the winter months, species such as Cormorants, gulls, geese, harriers, Starlings, thrushes and many of the small seed-eating perching birds form nighttime roosts, which can sometimes be easily monitored. The counts can be carried out either as the birds leave the roost at dawn, or as they arrive at dusk. Usually the birds enter and leave the roosts in relatively distinct flocks, which can be counted quite accurately. If the numbers involved are large, it is often a good idea to record the size of each flock into a pocket tape-recorder, so that you don't have to take your eyes off the birds to write notes. By recording the arrival and departure directions of the flocks, you will also be able to work out the main feeding areas of that particular roost; and doing this over a long period of time for adjacent roosts can provide a fascinating insight into the feeding habits of a particular species.

THE COMMON BIRDS CENSUS AND
RELATED SURVEYS

For birds which are widely distributed and common, such as many of the territorial songbirds which breed in Britain, it is impossible to count the whole population in a survey. Instead, sample areas must be counted, and the results extrapolated to the whole population, while repeat counts of the same area from month to month and year to year allow changes in population size to be monitored. Several techniques for monitoring species like this have been devised, each being appropriate for particular situations.

The best known of these techniques is the BTO's Common Birds Census, which is used to track the year-to-year fluctuations in popu-

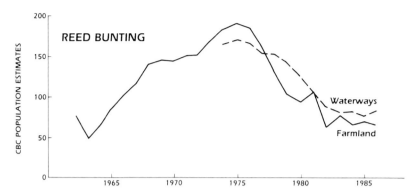

Common Birds Census and Waterways Bird Survey population estimates
for the Reed Bunting on farmland and along waterways respectively.
Breeding populations fall markedly after severe winters
and there has been a more systematic decline since the mid 1970s
as a result of changing agricultural practices.

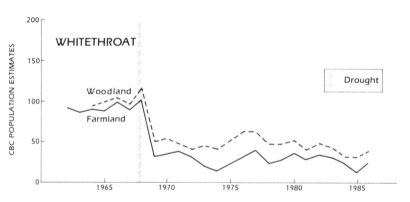

Common Birds Census population estimates for the Common Whitethroat
on farmland and woodland. Breeding populations declined
precipitously from 1969 as a result of drought
on its Sahel wintering grounds.

lation size of many of our songbirds. About two hundred bird-watchers conduct the survey each year on sample plots of woodland and farmland around the United Kingdom. The mapping technique used in this census is both demanding and rewarding. Each plot is visited about ten times in the breeding season, during which the observer maps the positions of all the birds seen or heard. Practising this so-called mapping technique is therefore an excellent way to brush up your ability to identify birds by sound, as well as by sight.

At the end of the breeding season participants submit their completed maps to the BTO, where individual species maps are constructed allowing the number of territories in each plot to be assessed. The results of the Common Birds Census are published annually and, as the long run of counts builds up, we can begin to understand the factors behind the changing fortunes of our songbirds.

The Waterways Birds Survey uses a method which is very similar to that of the Common Birds Census. Waterways and their birds are particularly sensitive to environmental change, and this survey monitors several species which are not covered by the Common Birds Census, such as Grey Wagtail, Dipper and Kingfisher.

Mapping techniques don't work on monotonous and extensive habitats such as moorland or extensive forests, because there are not enough landmarks to plot your observations accurately. Under these conditions, two other techniques can be used. Transect counts are made by surveying a fixed transect line across the habitat, recording the numbers of birds seen or heard within a certain distance of the line. By joining together the results from parallel transect lines, one can produce a sort of map. This technique works well for ground-nesting birds, such as breeding waders and game birds on moorland. Such species can be very reluctant to show themselves as an observer walks past, and the efficiency of a census can be improved by dragging a rope lightly over the surface of the ground between two observers, to flush the birds.

Point counts use a similar method, except that the counts are made from a number of fixed points rather than from a transect line. Usually the observer waits at the sample point for a period of, say, twenty minutes to record all the birds seen or heard. This method has the advantage of being relatively straightforward, whilst allowing a large area of habitat to be surveyed in a relatively short time.

COUNTING MIGRANTS

Visible migration probably fires greater excitement in more bird-watchers than does a good twitch! The very fact that the birds are migrating makes counting difficult unless the birds are all visibly moving in one direction past a known point. Sea-watching, the recording of migrating seabirds as they pass a headland, or the funnelled birds of prey migrations visible at Gibraltar or the Bosphorus, are good examples. Unfortunately, few of our migrants are as accommodating as this; instead, most of them migrate unobserved at night. How, then, do we know whether the Black-tailed Godwits at the sewage farm, or the Fieldfares on the sea buckthorn, are the same individuals as were there yesterday? To answer such questions requires very detailed fieldwork to measure the number of migrants passing through. Even though only a few birds may be present each day, the total number of individuals passing through a migration staging post may be very large. The bird observatories around our coasts have led the study of such migrations by combining detailed counts of the birds present each day with intensive ringing.

ON YOUR OWN PATCH

There is nowhere better to develop your birdwatching than on your own patch, at home! The secret is to get to know your area and its birds intimately, by making regular visits and keeping simple notes, so that you can track the changing fortunes of your local birds from month to month and year to year. The first stage in embarking on such a project, which may captivate your interests and spare time for many years to come, is to choose your study area. This will ideally be close to home and have good access the year round. It could be a local reservoir, a wood, a small estuary, a piece of river, coast or farmland; alternatively, you could study a square from the national Ordnance Survey Grid. In many counties the BTO operates a system whereby their members are allocated a 10-kilometre square of their own, and they are then responsible for carrying out all national surveys in that square. However, if you do not have the time or energy for such an extensive area, why not start by studying your garden birds? Even from your kitchen window you can follow the ups and downs of a surprising range of species – from summer migrants coming from south of the Sahara, to winter migrants from Scandinavia, as well as our own residents.

The only equipment needed for fieldwork are your binoculars (and perhaps a telescope for long-distance work), a map, a good recording notebook and a couple of pencils. The Ordnance Survey maps are excellent value, the most useful scale probably being the 1:25 000 series, which show all the major features that are likely to be relevant to the birds on your patch. Reading these maps is quite straightforward, but be especially careful to give the eastings (along the bottom!) before the northings (up the side!) in any grid reference. Always record the results of your fieldwork so that what you did can be interpreted later, even by someone else. Besides recording the date, time, location (place and county), map reference, weather and the number of each species counted, you should indicate if your count was incomplete and note the units in which you were counting (individuals seen, pairs, singing males, etc.).

Although most of us do no more with our birdwatching than

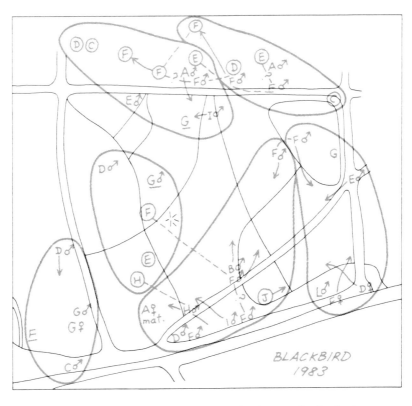

Common Birds Census map for Blackbirds, showing the distribution
of registrations and territories on a farmland plot in 1983.
The letters and symbols indicate visits and observations of
territorial behaviour.

enjoy it and submit a few records for someone else to analyse, there are a few hundred amateur ornithologists across Britain who devote much, if not all, of their spare time to the study of a particular species, site or ornithological problem. This sort of ornithology can be totally addictive and immensely rewarding – collecting your own set of data can open a completely new world of investigation.

Much of this effort goes to waste unless the results are written up. There are many scientific journals, such as *Bird Study*, *Ringing and Migration*, and *British Birds*, eager to help the amateur ornithologist publish his or her findings. It is not possible to cover here the sorts of analyses you could draw up from your data, but an excellent introduction for the keen ornithologist would be the BTO's guide *Statistics for Ornithologists*. This explains, step by step and using examples from real field studies, how to classify, analyse and present your hard-won data. From here, it is only a short step to writing your first scientific paper – a satisfying goal for any ornithologist!

JOINING IN WITH SURVEYS

The contribution that birdwatchers can make to research is nowhere greater than in Britain where there are sophisticated channels, through local bird clubs, the BTO and some other national organisations, for gathering bird data. Your county bird recorder will certainly be interested to receive your records for the county bird report and, by joining the BTO or your bird club, you will be able to find out which surveys are in progress. Every year, the BTO carries out national surveys of particular species, in addition to the long-term monitoring programmes already described; recent ones have been of Lapwings, Goosanders and Red-breasted Mergansers, Woodlarks, Ringed Plovers, Cirl Buntings, Mute Swans and Rooks. Species are usually chosen for surveys on the basis of conservation priority. The joy of most of these surveys is that they require you to do no more than to direct your birdwatching to particular species or habitats and to submit your observations centrally. Here, the observations of thousands of individual birdwatchers can be combined to show what is happening nationally.

An enormous amount of energy and resources is expended each year on bird surveys and monitoring programmes. What is the purpose of gathering all this information? Conservation is no longer a subject to be promoted just by the enlightened few, it has become an accepted form of land use, and an issue which is given high priority by government, planners and developers. Birds are widespread and abundant, conspicuous and popular; also, they are relatively easy to monitor and sensitive to a whole range of environmental changes from climate and pollutants, to habitat change and disturbance. Being high in the food chain, they are also very good indicators of the general health of the environment. Birds have therefore become an important factor in wildlife conservation. They have had a major impact on the selection of sites as nature reserves, in the designation of areas to receive special protection, and in the highlighting of issues such as the damaging effects of pesticides, acidification of upland rivers, afforestation of the Caithness Flows, and destruction of our hedgerows. Just as the effect of a development on noise levels, landscape and transport systems must be shown to be acceptable before planning permission is granted, so its impact on bird populations must be objectively measured. Indeed, legislation is shortly to be imposed in all EEC countries, making it compulsory for comprehensive environmental impact assessments to be undertaken for all significant developments. The need for information about our bird populations is likely to grow even more in the future. By joining the BTO, concerned birdwatchers can therefore make a direct contribution to all aspects of conservation in the countryside as a whole.

Curlews on tidal mudflats – any industrial development here could have a disastrous effect on their habitat.

5

MOVEMENTS AND MIGRATION: THE RINGER'S TALE

Chris Mead

BIRD MOVEMENTS

For many people the most fascinating aspect of birds' behaviour is their ability to move around the country – even the world – with consummate ease. In fact it is only in the last century that we have begun to realise the full extent of bird movements. Before that all sorts of theories were put forward to explain the ebb and flow of bird populations. Swallows and martins were thought to hibernate in the mud at the bottom of ponds. Aristotle believed that the summer Redstarts in Greece became Robins in the winter and that the Garden Warblers transmuted into Blackcaps. There was even an amazing theory that migrant birds flew upwards to spend the winter on the moon – published as a serious contribution to ornithology in 1703 by 'A Person of Learning and Piety'!

FROM KENT TO THE TRANSVAAL

We now know much better and realise that most bird species have evolved their own patterns of migration which allow them to use different areas at different times of the year. A typical but relatively simple example is that of Swallows which nest in a stable in the Home Counties during Britain's summer. They are able to raise a family (or even two or three broods) by feeding on flying insects from April through to early September. However, they could not possibly stay in Britain for the winter when the cold wipes out all their food. So they migrate southwards to spend the winter in southern Africa,

Swallows congregate in vast numbers at coastal reedbeds before they set off on migration. Their apparent disappearance after the night's roosting led early naturalists to wonder if they weren't hibernating in the mud.

finding plenty of flying insects in the shadow of Table Mountain or round the gold mines of the Transvaal.

This is a typical classical migration: a regular movement from one place to another *and back again*, taking place on an annual basis. In Britain we are well placed to see all sorts of birds moving backwards and forwards, east and west and north and south, at different times of the year. Different species, even different populations of the same species, have evolved strategies over thousands, even millions, of generations to suit their way of life and the areas available for them to live in. There is a single major reason for migration to have become so important for birds: the changing seasons. Because the availability of food changes dramatically as the weather gets colder or warmer, dryer or wetter, so birds develop different adaptations to exploit these conditions as efficiently as possible. If this means that they are unable to live in the same area all the year round, clearly they will have to move to an area where they are able to survive. Unravelling the resulting patterns of bird movements has now become an obsession for many birdwatchers.

AN OBSESSION WITH SPECIMENS

In Victorian times the main interest in birds was the collection of rare and interesting specimens to keep in cabinets as skins or stuffed birds. Many collectors came to realise that the rarest birds seemed to turn up on remote islands during autumn or spring – at the times of migration.

Some took to frequenting such places themselves, roaming the fields and cliff-tops with gun at the ready. Others put in 'standing orders', letting the local islanders know that they would be willing to pay for interesting specimens. It was also quickly realised that many birds were attracted to lighthouses and organised surveys were made of the birds coming to the lights in both Britain and Ireland. These studies established a baseline for the timing of passage migration around our coasts.

For many years ornithologists and general naturalists, like Gilbert White, had kept diaries of the ebb and flow of their local bird populations, recording the first summer migrants to be seen in spring – and the last ones in the autumn; when the first Redwings appeared in the fields and when the passage Greenshanks and

Common Sandpipers paid fleeting visits at the edges of the local ponds and streams. Gradually the patterns of bird movements through Britain became clearer.

However, this was not much use for answering the obvious questions of where they came from and went to. Gradually, scientists began to realise that the specimens coming from different areas of Europe and Africa included not only local non-migrant species but also others which looked exactly the same as birds found in other parts of the world at different times of the year. Thus the connections started to be made – Redwings shot in Finland in the summer belonged to the same species as those found in Britain, France and Spain in the autumn and winter.

THE FIRST RINGERS

With such crude and imprecise information, it was no easy task to sort out what was happening with species like many of the ducks, waders and warblers which have a very wide distribution and no local difference in plumage. It was then that the idea of marking birds first started. Several of the early schemes were not much use, for the leg rings that were used either did not have a unique identifying number or lacked a return address. But in 1899, scientific bird ringing started with the scheme run from Viborg in Denmark by Christian Mortensen. Other countries followed suit and, by 1930, most European countries had their own schemes.

In Britain two schemes started, almost simultaneously, during 1909. One was run from London by Harry Witherby, the proprietor of *British Birds* magazine; the other scheme was based in Aberdeen and was run by the young Landsborough Thomson – at the time only an undergraduate. The two schemes merged amicably after the First World War and in 1936, just a few years after its founding, the scheme was taken over by the British Trust for Ornithology.

By agreement with the Natural History Museum in South Kensington (where the office was housed for about twenty-five years), the address *Brit. Museum, LONDON SW7* is used on most rings. This is very important, for an address on a bird ring has to be instantly recognisable to a finder anywhere in the world – and to the Post Office, no matter where the letter is posted. One recent recovery in Nigeria, the first British House Martin reported from south of the Sahara,

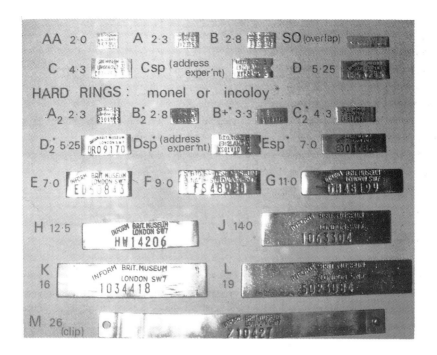

Flattened examples of the rings we now use in Britain. The hard metal rings are needed for the long-lived birds and those likely to wear down their rings on rocks and shingle.

almost failed to reach the BTO as the finder's writing made LONDON look like LOUZON. The intelligent Nigerian postman sent it to the Philippines (Louzon is the main island), where someone realised the mistake and posted it on to London. The recovery took five months to reach us – much slower than the House Martin's own journey time. On the smallest rings we have to use *BTO TRING, ENGLAND* or the letters would be too small to read. This rather enigmatic address actually loses something approaching 40% of all recoveries – who is Mr B. T. O. Tring and where in England does he live?

HOW RINGING WORKS

In principle, the idea behind ringing is simple. The ringer puts a numbered and addressed ring round a bird's leg and sends the ringing information in to the headquarters. Later on, another person (possibly a different ringer catching the bird alive) reports it to the headquarters. The two bits of information are matched up, and we know where that particular bird was at two distinct and precise moments in its life. The House Martin, for example, was ringed at Rye Meads, near Hoddesdon in Hertfordshire, on 10 September 1983. It was killed at Anambra in Nigeria, 5135 kilometres south of Hoddesdon, and reported in a letter dated 26 February 1984.

The leg of a bird is an ideal place to mark it. The rings are made of metal and split, so that they can be opened out and then closed round the leg with special pliers. They are not tight but can move up and down and rotate. The legs of even the largest species of birds have reached adult dimensions in the first few weeks of their lives, and the diameter varies very little indeed between individuals of the same species. It is therefore very easy to provide ringers with a series of different sizes of rings which will suit all the available species. The British rings start with an internal diameter of 2.0mm for the likes of Goldcrest, Willow Warbler and Wren and gradually increase in size to reach 26mm for swans and eagles. Taking into account different metals and special rings, thirty different types of ring are in use.

Holding the bird firmly in one hand, special pliers are used to close the ring around its leg.

TYPES OF RING

The type of metal used is most important in ensuring that the rings will do their job properly – they should mark the bird as an individual for life. This is quite easy with little songbirds that are not going to survive for many years anyway, but for a big, tough, long-lived seabird or wader it is almost impossible. Such birds live for twenty years or more and seem to spend most of their time trotting about in extremely abrasive conditions in shingle or on rocks. Modern rings are made of very sophisticated alloys (in the case of British rings, incoloy – based on nickel and chrome) which not only resist corrosion but are also very hard. The first hard material used (monel – based on copper and nickel) can withstand boiling concentrated acid but, when on the leg of a seabird in the tropics, corrodes very quickly. This was found to be due to tiny electric cells being formed in the crevices of the inscription in warm, salty water. In some cases terns came back from West Africa with holes punched right through their rings!

Now, many badly worn rings from birds like Guillemots and Razorbills can be read by passing an electric current across the ring to a piece of copper in a chemical solution as the pressure, at the time of stamping the number, will have altered the crystal structure of the metal. In the worst cases, the metal has been totally worn away; then, of course, there is no hope of finding out anything about the bird. Old birds are particularly important for detailed population studies as they will have made the biggest life-time contribution to the breeding population; unfortunately, the results from many early studies, where soft metals were used for the rings, were most unreliable.

FINDINGS OF THE PIONEER RINGERS

Such problems were far from the minds of the pioneer ringers. Essentially they were ringing birds to find out where they went. It must have been really thrilling in the early days to receive the first recovery of a British-ringed Swallow in South Africa. It was an adult female, ringed at Rosehill, Staffordshire, by J. R. B. Masefield (brother of the poet) on 6 May 1911 and reported from near Utrecht, in Natal, on 23 December 1913. Since then more than 400 have been

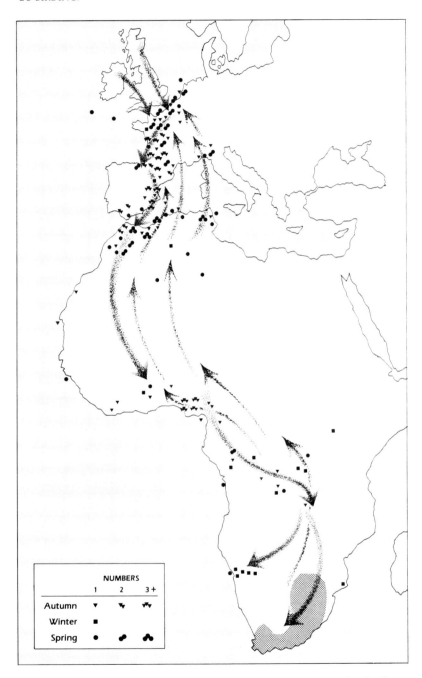

Migration routes for British swallows to and from their winter area in South Africa.

reported as making the journey to or from South Africa – including several caught by a ringer in Cape Province, operating within a mile of the southernmost point of the continent.

Such was the excitement generated by the early results that Harry Witherby announced, after the first three records of Lesser Black-backed Gull had been reported from Iberia, that ringers should concentrate on other species as 'we now know where this one goes'.

It soon became clear that ringing could show a great deal more about movements than could be understood from just a handful of records. For many species it is proving possible to unravel the precise timing and routes of movements, differences between the sexes, between birds of the same species from different areas, between youngsters and experienced adults and even between years when the weather patterns are not the same or food availability is altered. After a few years, it became clear that ringing would also cast light on the question of how long birds live.

Initially this was looked at only from the point of view of longevity – what was the oldest individual of the species so far recorded? However, at a famous meeting of the British Ornithologist's Club during the 1940s, David Lack presented an analysis he had made of recoveries of ringed Robins to discover what percentage survived from year to year. His result of 38% of adults and 28% of young birds was greeted with derision – his audience did not believe this could be right or dead birds would be scattered everywhere. The Chairman of the meeting, Landsborough Thomson, was his only supporter and, of course, they were quite right. It is easy to see why. A hundred adult Robins at the beginning of the breeding season will form fifty pairs, ninety per cent of which will have a couple of broods of two or three young at a time. So now there are one hundred adults and between two and three hundred youngsters alive. Unless there is quite a substantial reduction in the numbers of birds before the start of the next breeding season, Robin populations will start to increase very rapidly indeed!

MODERN RINGING SCHEMES

Computer analysis of ringing and recovery information is now used in the study of all aspects of change in bird populations. For example we might eventually hope to be able to discover, for a declining species, whether enough youngsters are surviving to replace lost adults or if the mortality rate among adult birds is putting the population at risk. Unfortunately these analyses are pretty tricky since experience has shown that the reporting rate (the likelihood of a bird being reported if it dies) varies within the same species from year to year, and that mortality rates also vary, both from year to year and between the sexes and different ages. Within a few years most major schemes will be seeking to computerise not only the recovery data but also information on the individual birds being ringed.

HOW YOU CAN JOIN IN

In Britain the National Ringing Scheme is run by the British Trust for Ornithology from its Headquarters in Tring. There are well over 2000 licensed ringers, most of whom are already trained to operate by themselves. The BTO insists on comprehensive training. Standards are kept very high not only to protect the birds but also because the scientific value of the whole scheme would be jeopardised if the data being gathered were compromised. The object is to find out what healthy, wild birds do naturally. If the process of handling and ringing them, or the ring itself, were to harm the birds the whole operation would be pointless.

The legal basis of the scheme is the Wildlife and Countryside Act (1981), which allows the Nature Conservancy Council to licence people for the ringing of birds. The NCC also makes a substantial contribution to the cost of the scheme. However, the bulk of the money for payment of salaries, purchase of rings and equipment comes from the ringers themselves. Most are recruited from the ranks of amateur birdwatchers, from all walks of life, who are members of the BTO.

TRAINING TO BE A RINGER

Ringing courses, run over a whole week or just a weekend, are not the way to learn the rudiments of ringing. To do this potential recruits are put in touch with an active ringer who lives near them or, if this is not possible, recommended to stay at a Bird Observatory. On the courses details of age and sex determination and other more

Measurements of birds caught for ringing help to establish their
condition (weight). Sometimes the sex of the bird can be determined
by measuring the length of its bill.

specialised aspects are demonstrated but, at the very start, a new
ringer needs to be taught how to hold a bird safely, take its measurements and put on the ring. What generally happens is that the begin-
ner first handles birds which have already been dealt with, so that it
doesn't matter if he or she releases the bird by mistake. After a few
sessions it will become obvious to the trainer if the recruit has the
makings of a ringer and then is the time that a commitment, on both
sides, needs to be made.

This commitment has to be genuine, for the training process, to
obtain a full permit, will generally take some years of pretty intensive
effort. The average applicant for a full A or B permit will have ringed
or handled several thousand birds before being recommended by his
trainer. Most ringers are able to achieve C permit status, which
enables them to use their trainer's rings by themselves at their
trainer's discretion, after a couple of years. Although training is
always given by particularly well-experienced ringers, many ringers
work together in ringing groups. These are often based on particular
sites where most of their ringing takes place. Some concentrate on
particular species within an area – for example, the Wash Wader
Ringing Group which has marked huge numbers of waders round
the Wash over a period of almost thirty years.

Of course, the first problem, whether for raw trainee or fully qualified ringer, is to lay hands on the bird. When ringing first started in Britain, the emphasis was on ringing nestlings. It is easy to ring large numbers of young gulls in a colony, at the right time of the year; but, unless you are an ace nest-finder, ringing of nestling songbirds is a very time-consuming and soul-destroying process. In many areas predators such as cats, Magpies and Crows destroy the majority of the nests before the chicks are old enough to be ringed. In any case, the chicks of most small open-nesting birds are only in the nest for twelve or thirteen days. For the first five their legs are too small to take the rings and, after day nine or ten, they may explode prematurely from the nest if disturbed. There is thus only a period of three or four days when the ringer can safely ring them.

One way of increasing the numbers of nestlings ringed, of hole-nesting species, is to put up nest-boxes. Over the years many ringers have done this; and enormous numbers of young tits and Pied Flycatchers, in particular, are ringed each year. In several areas, the activity of ringers with their nest-boxes has clearly increased the local populations of Pied Flycatchers and even helped them spread into areas where they used hardly, if ever, to nest. The ringing of chicks is particularly useful as one knows exactly how old the birds are and where they came from. Many special studies of particular populations of birds rely on the blanket ringing of the local nestlings for their data. These run through almost the whole range of species, from Red-throated Divers, Grey Herons, various waders and sea-birds to many different songbirds.

CATCHING THE BIRDS

For most of the year there are no nestlings available and the ringer's wits must be pitted against the intelligence and guile of free-flying, fully grown birds. In some countries the ringing schemes started whilst bird-catching for food or for caging was still in operation. For example in Belgium, the Netherlands and Italy some fowling yards, where such catchers operated, have been converted for use by ringers. In Britain such practices stopped many years before ringers began to operate in any numbers, and over the years the ringers have had to rediscover and invent their own techniques.

Some methods used with great success in the past cannot be employed as they are too dangerous – pole traps that catch birds of prey by the legs, or sticky bird-lime, are outlawed. A few examples are set out below – the last three (Helgoland traps, cannon nets and mist nets) are the ones most commonly used nowadays. Anyone training to become a general ringer now will undoubtedly be taught how to use mist nets. This is the main method of catching small- to medium-sized birds up to the size of a Blackbird.

Duck decoys

These are long, curved funnels, covered in netting, radiating from a central pond. By showing a stuffed fox or weasel from behind screens (or using a trained dog, traditionally called Piper), the inquisitive ducks are lured down the funnel until the decoy man can scare them right into it and into the bag at the tapered end. Decoys are still used by the Wildfowl Trust for ringing at Peakirk, near Peterborough, and at their headquarters at Slimbridge on the Severn. When the ducks are caught, ringed and released the annual catches are much smaller than when they are being killed – clearly the released birds either warn the others or put them off by their reluctance to enter the pipe again.

Chardonneret

This is a small automatic trap with a roof entrance: when it is set, a bird entering and standing on the perch causes the lid to close. It was traditionally used for catching finches by having a caged decoy below the trap. Ringers are not allowed to use captive decoys, so, nowadays, the traps are generally baited with peanuts for tits and finches. *Chardonneret* is the French name for the Goldfinch.

Potter

This is a floor entrance automatic trap named after a ringer, Miss J. A. Potter. The size of the trap determines what it will catch. Small ones are good for finches, Robins, Dunnocks, chats; bigger ones will take Blackbirds and other thrushes. Even bigger and, if you are really lucky, a Jay might go in.

House trap

This is basically a box with various funnel entrances through which the birds can get in but find it difficult to get out. Some ringers have made them with drop doors, too. Keen gardeners have been known to have fruit cages which convert into house traps outside the fruit season! The birds are not easy to catch, even once they are in the trap, unless there is a catching box and ramp in one corner.

Clap net

With this a frame net is carried over the birds whilst they are on the ground. Small nets are pulled over by the operator, but bigger ones need elastic or a spring to power them over so quickly that the birds cannot escape. Big sets of clap nets – doubles, with one firing towards the other – were the traditional means of catching birds in the fowling yards. Skilled operators were not only able to catch huge numbers of migrants such as finches, pipits, larks and buntings coming to investigate their decoy birds but they were also able to snatch falcons and other birds of prey out of the sky as they stooped on the decoys. A useful source of extra revenue!

Cannon nets

These are essentially clap nets without the poles. Instead the netting is carried over the birds by projectiles fired by explosive over their heads. The crucial safety factors of this system in operation are three-fold: first there should be no birds actually standing on or beside the net, secondly there should be none in the air, where the net is being fired across, and, most important, the charge should be sufficient to get the net out really fast to its full extent where it then falls on the birds. This method is particularly useful for catching difficult species such as geese, waders and gulls.

Helgoland trap

This is named after an island in the North Sea off Germany. Here special hedges were allowed to grow thick and dense, and netting was placed along them to catch migrant birds for food. The idea was adapted to become a huge funnel of wire netting, over some attractive cover, down which the birds could be driven by the ringers into a catching box. Almost all the Bird Observatories still have one or two in operation as they are unaffected by the wind and can also be operated in moderately wet conditions. The most developed examples were at the Baltic ringing station at Rossiten where the biggest one was over 100 feet (30 metres) wide and about 30 feet (9 metres) high at the entrance. The shape is crucial, since the birds should see netting all round them if they try to break back but an apparently clear escape route through the glazed catching box.

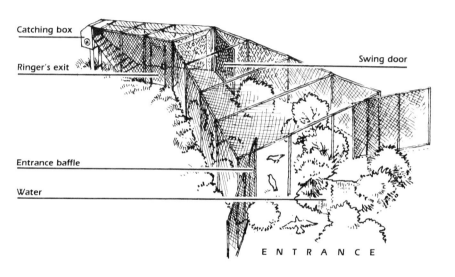

Catching box

Ringer's exit

Swing door

Entrance baffle

Water

E N T R A N C E

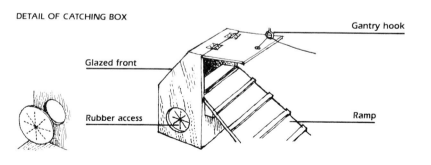

DETAIL OF CATCHING BOX

Gantry hook

Glazed front

Rubber access

Ramp

Helgoland traps are the classic Bird Observatory traps. Their main advantage is that they are workable in weather conditions that defeat more sophisticated devices.

Mist nets

Unlike the cannon nets which were traditionally used for catching waders for eating, mist nets, when properly used, are a very safe means of catching all sorts of small- to medium-sized birds. The cannon nets depended on the quarry becoming tangled in the meshes. Mist nets are stretched between tall poles, trapping any bird which flies into them. Originally they were made of silk but now fine nylon or polyester thread is used. The standard lengths of net in use range from 6 to 18 metres and they are set 3 metres high.

Mist nets were invented in Japan in the Middle Ages and used for centuries for catching birds for food and for caging. Happily they were not introduced to Britain until they were discovered by a senior American officer, who was a bander (ringer) of long standing, at the end of World War Two and have only been available to bird ringers.

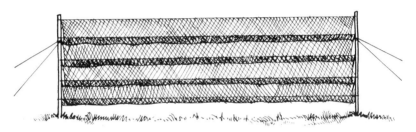

Mist nets are light, portable and highly effective.

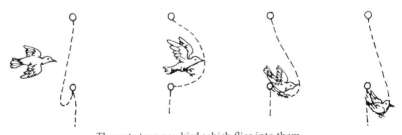

The nets trap any bird which flies into them.

IDENTIFICATION

Having captured the bird, the first job for the ringer is to identify it. This is not always easy, for there are a surprising number of species which are very similar. For instance, only very tiny differences in the wing structure will enable the ringer to tell whether he is dealing with a Chiffchaff, Willow or Wood Warbler.

The ring can then be fitted. It is here that the crucial detective work of the ringer starts, for each bird ringed is much more useful if it can be accurately aged and sexed. This involves looking closely at the plumage for features which distinguish old and young, male and female of the species in question.

There are certain techniques which are widely applicable. For instance, in many species only the adult birds undergo a full moult in the autumn and youngsters have a partial one. This means that throughout the rest of the year, if you can distinguish a mixture of old and new plumage, the bird must be a youngster. For many species, during the breeding season the shape of the cloaca of the males and females differ and often it is only the female which will fully develop a complete brood patch. There are various guides to help ringers through these problems.

WHAT HAS BEEN LEARNED FROM RINGING

Once examination of the bird is complete and the data recorded, it is released. However, the ringing is useless unless the full information is recorded and sent to the headquarters. Here it is filed in ring number order for, when the bird is reported by a member of the public, there is very little chance that the species will be known. In fact the most likely way in which the bird will be heard of again is when the original ringer re-traps it at the same site. Each year roughly 750 000 birds are ringed and it is estimated that more than 100 000 of them will be retrapped, at the original site, with the details kept solely in the ringer's own files. Some 14 000 or so will be recovered – that is, either found by a member of the public and reported to the BTO at Tring or recaptured by another ringer some distance from the original ringing site.

For each one of these 14 000 birds, a full recovery history is prepared on the BTO computer and the ringer and the finder are informed of it. Towards the end of 1986, the 400 000th recovery was reported and soon, at some time during 1988, the 20 000 000th bird will have been ringed in Britain. The table shows the top 25 in the overall ringing and recovery stakes at the end of 1985, the last year for which the lists have been prepared.

Numbers of Birds Ringed

(Figures in italics relate to birds outside the 'Top 25')

1 125 113					Blackbird
				187 926	Blackcap
				213 498	Black-headed Gull
1 370 549					Blue Tit
				36 911	*Canada Goose*
			482 840		Chaffinch
				37 321	*Cormorant*
				281 369	Dunlin
			416 747		Dunnock
		580 922			Great Tit
	882 220				Greenfinch
				205 583	Herring Gull
			354 781		House Sparrow
				96 973	*Lesser B-backed Gull*
				279 791	Linnet
				134 776	*Mallard*
				248 825	Manx Shearwater
				42 324	*Mute Swan*
				86 697	*Oystercatcher*
				11 850	*Pink-footed Goose*
				233 255	Reed Bunting
				253 455	Reed Warbler
			423 332		Robin
	662 232				Sand Martin
				293 750	Sedge Warbler
				117 143	*Shag*
			428 834		Song Thrush
952 756					Starling
				205 592	Storm Petrel
910 215					Swallow
				69 201	*Teal*
				183 546	Tree Sparrow
		583 464			Willow Warbler
				216 211	Wren

NUMBERS OF BIRDS RECOVERED

(Figures in italics relate to birds outside the 'Top 25')

Blackbird					41742
Blackcap	*1052*				
Black-headed Gull		10000			
Blue Tit			14049		
Canada Goose		7439			
Chaffinch	4095				
Cormorant	6190				
Dunlin	4435				
Dunnock	4220				
Great Tit	5508				
Greenfinch				18640	
Herring Gull			13356		
House Sparrow	5871				
Lesser B-backed Gull	6101				
Linnet	*1704*				
Mallard				22523	
Manx Shearwater	3526				
Mute Swan			14404		
Oystercatcher	5450				
Pink-footed Goose	3493				
Reed Bunting	*1478*				
Reed Warbler	*3018*				
Robin	6972				
Sand Martin			13092		
Sedge Warbler	*1537*				
Shag		8151			
Song Thrush		10965			
Starling					32403
Storm Petrel	*2400*				
Swallow	6668				
Teal				12351	
Tree Sparrow	*752*				
Willow Warbler	*1413*				
Wren	*1062*				

BTO 1985

Comparing the two lists you can see that it is not necessarily the species with the most birds ringed that produce the most recoveries. The recovery rate for a species depends on the size and conspicuousness of the bird and the likelihood of it dying where it might be found. Of all species, the Mute Swan has the highest recovery rate – for 42 324 ringed there have, so far, been 14 404 reports: a rate of more than thirty-four per cent. But then there are few birds bigger and more conspicuous than a Mute Swan and they are likely to die in places where someone will have to 'clear them up'. Going to the other extreme 583 464 Willow Warblers have produced only 1413 reports (0.24%); but then one can hardly find a much smaller bird and, for half the year, they are all in the depths of the African bush. Two other small birds, Chiffchaff and Goldcrest, have recovery rates of about 0.33% which can probably be accounted for because they are not trans-Saharan migrants and are therefore slightly more likely to be found and reported during the winter.

The overall recovery rate for birds ringed is 2.24%. This falls somewhere between Song Thrush and Greenfinch and most ordinary garden birds have rates between 1% and 3%. Birds with high recovery rates include the quarry species like ducks (Mallard 16.7% and Teal 17.8%), pest species which are frequently shot (Cormorant 16.6% and Woodpigeon 8.7%) and a few specials like Barn Owl (16.4%) and Tawny Owl (7.7%).

Obviously the recoveries reported can be used for all sorts of purposes. The fact that a bird has not moved a long way, or survived a long time, does not mean that its record is not important. It is only by gathering all the records together that it is possible to start working out what the average birds within the population do. For instance it can be shown that different species are at risk at different times of the year – even when they seem to be very similar.

Plotting the number of Bullfinch and Greenfinch records received each month immediately shows that the spring is a time of great stress for the Greenfinch. More recoveries are reported in March, April and May than at any other time of the year. For Bullfinch there is a distinct trough in the numbers of birds reported at this period. There is an easy explanation for this: the Bullfinch can digest fruit buds so it has a source of food available at a time when the ripe seeds needed by the Greenfinch are in very short supply.

It is also possible to look at the different reasons for recovery reported to see how the different species are affected. This is not as simple as it looks because clearly the recovery method will have a very big effect on whether the bird is reported or not – 'killed by cat and body proudly brought indoors onto the fireside mat' is a common report; 'unfortunate bird fell down dead of the palsy whilst roosting in the depths of a thick bush', is not. Amongst the seabirds the recoveries clearly show which species are at most risk from oiling – undoubtedly the auks and particularly the Guillemot.

However, the most interesting comparisons are within species. Traffic accidents, for instance, account for 20.8% of male Blackbirds reported but only 12.8% of females; on the other hand, cats take 21.0% of reported females and only 16.9% of males. There is an easy explanation – cars tend to be the downfall of males defending their territories (or trying to encroach on their neighbour's), whereas cats are quite likely to take an incubating female from the nest. One can also see how young birds learn about the world. Analysis of the Swallow recoveries reveals that 37.8% of the youngsters reported within a month of leaving the nest had died in traffic accidents; for the next year or so the rate went down to 12.7%; and for experienced adults, the rate was reduced further to 7.3%.

The most thrilling recoveries are, of course, those which show birds living a very long time or travelling a long way. Some of the record individuals for a selection of species are shown in the following tables. Each year the longevity records for twenty or thirty species are being beaten since, until the early 1960s, most rings were made of a rather soft material and a number of species have had hard rings for rather less than their potential life-span.

The second table gives the maximum distance so far recorded, for birds ringed in Britain and Ireland. The three species with records of 16 000 kilometres or more (Manx Shearwater, Arctic Tern and Common Tern) were all found in Australia. Otherwise the movements of 10 000 kilometres or more are birds which have made it to the far south of Africa. The Pochard and Ruff are far to the east in the Soviet Union and the Mallard went westwards to Canada. Many of the summer migrants have chalked up movements of about 5000 kilometres which takes them well across the Sahara and just about to the equator (if they were ringed in southern Britain).

In many ways the birds that do *not* move are just as interesting. It comes as no real surprise that none of the Red Grouse, Marsh Tits

LONG-LIVED INDIVIDUALS

AGE (YEARS)

Species	Age (years)
Arctic Tern	26.96
Blackbird	14.79
Black-headed Gull	21.58
Blue Tit	12.36
Buzzard	15.91
Chaffinch	11.60
Collared Dove	16.13
Curlew	23.77
Dunlin	15.78
Eider	26.02
Fulmar	25.07
Gannet	24.54
Grey Heron	18.49
Grey Plover	17.87
Greylag Goose	18.68
Guillemot	24.87
Lesser B-backed Gull	24.32
Mallard	20.94
Manx Shearwater	29.93
Mute Swan	23.58
Oystercatcher	24.53
Pied Wagtail	9.91
Puffin	27.22
Razorbill	24.99
Reed Warbler	10.83
Robin	8.42
Rook	18.35
Shag	22.93
Starling	22.07
Storm Petrel	18.04
Swallow	15.98
Swift	15.91
Tawny Owl	16.95
Yellowhammer	11.84

LONG-DISTANCE TRAVELLERS

DISTANCE (KM)

Arctic Tern				18056
Common Tern				17641
Manx Shearwater				16675
Storm Petrel			10839	
Arctic Skua			10475	
Sandwich Tern			10467	
Swallow			10417	
Spotted Flycatcher			10015	
Knot			9921	
Ruff			9582	
Swift			9367	
Pochard			9257	
Great Skua		8046		
Mallard		7854		
Black-headed Gull	5689			
Sedge Warbler	5523			
Ringed Plover	5394			
Garden Warbler	5370			
Cuckoo	5368			
Gannet	5301			
Willow Warbler	5272			
Yellow Wagtail	4822			
White-fronted Goose	4728			
Sand Martin	4721			
Redstart	4718			
Fulmar	4687			
Redwing	4365			
Puffin	4074			
Starling	3458			
Siskin	3141			
Robin	2606			
Kestrel	2592			
Blackbird	2392			
Chaffinch	2257			

Great Tit	1446
Shag	1440
Rock Pipit	1359
Goldcrest	1292
Mute Swan	1080
Blue Tit	573
House Sparrow	444
Buzzard	436
Bullfinch	392
Yellowhammer	344
Long-tailed Tit	338
Tawny Owl	137
Magpie	137
Dipper	69
Marsh Tit	59
Red Grouse	26

SPEED RECORDS

	TIME (DAYS)	DISTANCE (KM PER DAY)
ARCTIC TERN	2	360
BAR-TAILED GODWIT	5	732
BLACKBIRD	2	412
BLACKCAP	3	280
COMMON SANDPIPER	4	297
DUNLIN	4	363
KNOT	8	651
MANX SHEARWATER	17	568
PIED FLYCATCHER	4	313
REDSHANK	1	391
REDWING	3	815
REED WARBLER	4	278
RING OUZEL	1	579
SAND MARTIN	4	309
SEDGE WARBLER	3	271
SPOTTED FLYCATCHER	3	349
STORM PETREL	1	284
SWALLOW	4	411
TEAL	1	813
TURNSTONE	1	597
WHEATEAR	2	471
WHITETHROAT	3	322
WIGEON	2	292
WILLOW WARBLER	3	433

or Dippers so far found have travelled more than 100 kilometres, nor that birds like the Yellowhammer, Bullfinch and Buzzard are pretty steadfastly stay-at-home. Some of the other species, with movements recorded in the range of 1000 to 2000 kilometres, are quite well-established migrants making an East–West flight in the autumn from Scandinavia, Finland and the western edge of the Soviet Union.

Associated with the distance movements, but depending even more on luck in fast reporting, are the speed records. These depend on the ringer marking the bird whilst it is moving or very shortly before it sets off and the unfortunate bird being found either on its journey or soon after it has arrived. Some of the twenty-four examples given are really amazing. For instance the Redwing was marked in a Midlands garden at the beginning of the cold weather of January 1963 and arrived, three days later, on the deck of a ship on its way eastwards across the Atlantic. It had responded to the bad weather by flying west for better conditions but had made the crucial mistake of missing Ireland! Its speed of 815 kilometres per day remains the record, although the Teal which travelled 813 kilometres in a single day came a close second. The next fastest was a Bar-tailed Godwit caught on its way down to the wintering area used by many of these waders on the Banc d'Arguin in Senegal. The only other bird averaging more than 25 kilometres per hour was a young Knot, from the Siberian population, ringed on the Wash in September and found eight days later in West Africa! However, one particular Manx Shearwater deserves a very special mention: it was ringed as a nestling on Skokholm, the seabird island off South Wales, and found, two and a half weeks later, on the wintering grounds in the South Atlantic off South America.

SOME CASE STUDIES

We have learnt a great deal about the migration routes and strategy of some of our birds as a direct consequence of ringing. The results come not only from the dedicated work of generations of registered ringers but also from the unsung heroes of ringing – the finders who send in the details. Were it not for them we would only be able to make the connections between places where registered ringers were operating. So, even if you do not want to participate in the ringing of birds please always look out for rings on any corpses brought in by the cat, washed up on the beach or squashed on the road.

A very small proportion of ringed birds have escaped from aviaries and we will not be able to trace them, but the vast majority have come from various ringing schemes scattered throughout Britain and Europe. Whatever the origin of the ring, we will do our utmost to trace the full ringing details if you send in the finding information to:

> The Ringing Office
> British Trust for Ornithology
> Beech Grove
> Tring
> Herts HP23 5NR

The information required from the finder is the ring number and the details of the return address. We also need to know when and where you found it. If you have any idea what the bird was please let us know but, even more important, how did you find it? Was the bird dead, fresh or skeletal? Had it been run over by a car, caught by a cat, drowned in a water butt, collided with wires? And, finally, who are you – we cannot send you details of the ringing of the bird if we do not know who you are. If the bird is alive and fit, please release it having made absolutely certain that you have the number recorded correctly. If it is alive but sick or injured try to get it to an expert who can look after it – there are good bird hospitals scattered throughout the country and they can often be contacted through the RSPCA or the local police. If the bird is dead, return the ring securely sellotaped to the letter and with the number mentioned in the letter too – many rings get punched out of their envelopes by the Post Office franking machines. If you would like the ring back as a souvenir, this can be arranged – but whatever you do, do not stick it on another bird!

From time to time there are special surveys which involve colour-ringing birds so that they can be distinguished, as individuals, in the field without having to be caught again. The Ringing Office will try to trace such birds if you have a sighting but it is very important to note exactly which rings were on which legs, what the order of them was and any engraved inscriptions visible on them. Use of a telescope is often essential. A few skilled observers are able to read the ring numbers on birds like Black-headed Gulls coming to eat bread on the seafront. This is pretty difficult to do accurately, as it is vital that the whole ring number is correctly recorded *and* that you know which scheme ringed it (that is, what the address on the ring was).

SWALLOW

This is the small bird which has produced the great majority of South African ringing recoveries from British marking. In the autumn, Swallows migrate across the Channel, down through western France and across Spain to reach Africa somewhere along the Moroccan coast. This part of the migration is fairly gradual but they have a tough crossing of the western end of the Sahara to make before reaching the sub-tropical areas of Ghana or Nigeria.

Swallows from Britain winter mostly in South Africa, with a few in Namibia. They reach the wintering area at the end of October and may, sometimes, be caught out by late spring frosts in early November. If this happens there can be heavy mortality. British birds are joined by Russian ones from the area round the Urals. Other western European breeding populations do not go so far south.

The return migration starts in late February and the route back is further to the east than the autumn one. The Saharan crossing is also much tougher, as the desert is wider further to the east and there may be quite dry conditions along the northern edge. Tired, newly arrived birds at the northern oases may be very light but they seem to be able to recover if they are able to rest for a while and there is food available. Generally, Swallows first arrive in southern England around 15 April and the whole migration – roughly 9000 kilometres – probably takes between forty-five and sixty days in all.

SAND MARTIN

Intensive ringing during the 1960s charted the routes of Sand Martins out of Britain and on through Europe in great detail. Within Britain birds from colonies in the west of the country tend to funnel out through Sussex, but eastern and northern populations go out through East Anglia and Kent. The migrating birds may rest overnight in the unoccupied holes at colonies but many birds join together in huge

roosts in reed beds or willows – one such roost in the Fens was estimated to have peaked at 2 000 000 birds.

Unlike the Swallows, Sand Martins do not migrate far south of the Sahara and spend the winter in the Sahel zone just to the south of the desert. This is the area where the drought conditions have been so bad over the last twenty years and British Sand Martin populations crashed to about 7% of the mid-1960s population in 1984 and

Sand Martins breed communally in holes they make themselves in sandy banks.

1985. Since then there have been better rains in the Sahel and a slight recovery in numbers has been noted.

Unlike the Swallows, which rely on man's buildings for nesting sites, the Sand Martin, over much of southern Britain, relies completely on quarries and pits for suitable nesting places. Happily most workers at such pits are very fond of 'their' birds and provide excellent unofficial protection for them.

WILLOW WARBLER

This tiny bird is probably the most numerous small summer migrant to reach the northern areas of the Old World. The British and Irish population alone probably numbers some 20 000 000 birds at the start of the autumn migration. Typically, in mid-July, young birds appear all over the place as they explore the area near where they were hatched – probably working out where they will settle to breed next spring.

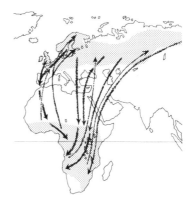

Willow Warblers defend individual breeding territories.

Their migration starts with a flight southwards to northern Iberia. They can do this without having to put on very much weight but, once they have reached northern Spain or Portugal, they then fatten up to reach roughly 11g (compared with a lean weight of 7g). This amount of fuel will allow them to make their next migratory flight of about forty-eight hours non-stop across the rest of Iberia, the Mediterranean, North Africa and the Sahara, so that they end up in the Sahel or the temperate open woodland just to its south.

They have not yet finished for they almost certainly move even further south. For instance, over wide areas of Zimbabwe during the northern winter, there are probably more Willow Warblers than all other species combined! Spring migration reverses this pattern and, as with the Swallows, tends to be along a rather more easterly route.

PIED FLYCATCHER

The Pied Flycatcher breeds in many parts of northern Europe but, in Britain, is a bird of the south-west peninsula, Wales, the Lake District and parts of Scotland and the north-eastern moors. Other populations breed in forest areas throughout Scandinavia and Finland as far east as Moscow (and even further).

All these birds migrate to winter in western Africa, mostly in the moist forests along the Gulf of Guinea coast. In order to get there they come westwards to fatten up in north-west Iberia. Here numerous recoveries of birds from all the areas where Pied Flycatchers have been ringed have been reported. The birds put on 65% or 70% fat and, like the Willow Warblers, make a single non-stop flight lasting two days or more direct to the wintering area – or close to it.

The return passage in spring does not go anywhere near north-western Iberia. That area is totally unsuitable at that time of year as it is still cold, wet and windy. The adult birds are desperate to get back on the breeding grounds as quickly as possible, for it is the early

A male Pied Flycatcher, at home in an oak wood.

birds that will have the best breeding sites, the biggest clutches and raise the most chicks.

BARNACLE GEESE

It has been known for many years that this species has several separate wintering areas in north-western Europe.

In the west, the population breeding in north-east Greenland winters in the Hebrides and along the west coast of Ireland. The Spitzbergen birds form the famous Solway flock. Although these two groups are only about an hour's flight apart, there is little mixing between them. Birds from Novaya Zemlya and Kolguev winter in the Netherlands; and the most easterly birds go to Hungary, the Black Sea, the Euphrates marshes and other Asiatic sites.

Barnacle and other geese migrate in family groups.

This tradition is rigidly passed on from parent to offspring as the birds undertake their first migration in family parties. It is clearly most important that this segregation should be properly understood before any plans which might disrupt the ecology of the separate wintering areas are undertaken.

KITTIWAKE

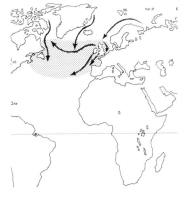

This attractive and delicate-looking small gull nests in colonies on cliffs. It is a real globe-trotter, with young birds from British colonies regularly being reported from the seas around Greenland and Newfoundland. In the past many of them were killed by the Grand Banks fishermen who used them as bait on their long-lines to catch cod. Their name for them is 'ticklelace', just as good a name from their call as 'kittiwake'.

After this long-distance movement in the immature phase of its life, the adult Kittiwake does not wander so far away. However, it is well adapted to a life at sea and goes out into the open oceans, outside the breeding season, just as happily as it lives much closer inshore when there are young in the nest to feed. This is a species that can be storm-driven in large numbers – onshore gales may pile up thousands, even tens of thousands, giving spectacular seawatching for birders.

GUILLEMOT

This seabird breeds in vast colonies at remote cliff sites. The adult birds have now been shown to attend the breeding ledges for most of the year. They certainly start coming ashore in October probably because it is very important, for their breeding success, for them to defend the most favoured ledges. This means that they do not migrate far for the winter. However, the young birds move quite long distances, winter-

Guillemots use their wings underwater, too.

ing much further afield than the adults, until they too become part of the breeding population.

There is good evidence to show that a parent, flightless because of its moult, may swim with the part-grown (and flightless) chick across the North Sea from the east coast colonies of Scotland to the Norwegian coast during late July and August. Shetland birds move further up Norway to spend the first part of the winter off the Lofoten Islands. Southern Welsh youngsters move up the Channel and so on. The understanding of these complicated patterns is very important for a species like the Guillemot, which is particularly vulnerable to oil spillages.

ARCTIC TERN

This is the migrant to beat them all. Arctic Terns from the high Arctic breeding colonies migrate southwards to winter off the Antarctic pack ice. These birds undoubtedly

An Arctic Tern – migrant superstar!

see more daylight in the course of a single year than any other living creature – except possibly a few privileged scientists.

They do not hang around and there are ringing recoveries of Scottish-ringed Arctic Tern chicks in West Africa within a month of fledging and some in South Africa after they have only been able to fly for about six weeks. The most southerly recovery of a British ring was a Farne Islands (Northumberland) Arctic Tern which crashed into the wheel-house of a Japanese whaler off the Antarctic pack ice.

Other terns are not generally so mobile, with Sandwich Terns spread round the African coast from the north round the Cape of Good Hope to Mozambique. Common Terns have mostly been found off West African coasts and Roseates seem to home in on Ghana. West African birds are often caught by children, both for fun and for food, and there is an education campaign, masterminded by the RSPB, to try to stop these losses.

KNOT

This bird breeds in the high Arctic. It migrates through Britain in large numbers and also winters on our major estuaries. In some years significant numbers of the Siberian breeding population pass through but, usually, it is the Greenland and Canadian populations that pass through or winter in Britain.

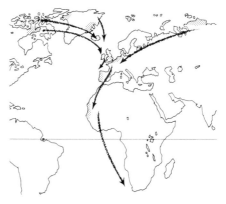

Peak counts and detailed studies of bird movements show that estuaries are of supreme importance to this and other coastal wader species. Not only are there very substantial wintering populations, but there are others which use Britain as a regular moulting site in the autumn. In addition huge numbers, both from our own winter population and also from further south, rely on British estuaries, particularly those round the Irish Sea, to fatten up during late April and May for the long journey towards the breeding grounds.

OSPREY

The return to Scotland of the Osprey as a breeding bird has been carefully monitored. We know that some of the original colonisers came from Swedish populations (they were already ringed). We also know that several of the young birds, fully protected and looked after in Britain, migrated southwards only to be shot either in the Mediterranean area on passage or in West Africa where they were wintering.

Mapping the recoveries from Scottish ringing, and from Norway, Sweden and Finland, is very instructive. The British birds have all been found in the winter on the very western edge of the Guinea Coast. Those from Sweden and Norway are spread all along that coast, and the Finnish ones extend as far as the Red Sea coast.

Recoveries and sightings of young, non-breeding Ospreys during the summer show that they wander around a great deal; and it is presumably this which has helped the splendid spread of breeding within Scotland. The migrating birds pass through England and it is surely just a matter of time before they begin to breed again south of the border.

WHITE STORK

Although not truly a British bird (it was last recorded breeding in Edinburgh in the fifteenth century), the White Stork is another classic migrant. It is adapted for soaring flight and is therefore constrained to take the short sea crossings. Hence the migration is funnelled through Gibraltar in the west and through the Bosphorus in the east. The record number of birds for the

White Stork migration is recorded as long ago as the Bible.

eastern route is roughly a third of a million in one autumn (roughly ten times the number seen on the western route).

White Storks are only able to migrate when the ground has warmed up in the sun and the updraughts have started to rise. This is a very efficient way of flying, as the effort required to keep the wings out-stretched and exercise control is roughly 3% of that needed for sustained flapping flight – something White Storks are capable of doing, with reluctance, only in short bouts.

The birds continue down into Africa and on the eastern route migrate all the way to South Africa. They are a familiar sight in the southern summer, quartering open ground for the large insects, amphibians and small mammals on which they feed. In some areas they are also known to prey on locust hoppers.

SHELDUCK

This handsome coastal duck undertakes a very particular migration, with most of the members of the species from all over north-west Europe going to the mudflats of the Helgoland Bight to moult in the autumn. In fact the breeding adults abandon their youngsters to 'aunties' who look after them in large creches.

Most European Shelduck moult in the SE North Sea.

A number of other species of wildfowl are known to migrate to moult. One of the northern estuaries in Norway has a huge flock of moulting Goosanders each autumn. In Britain Canada Geese, from a wide area of the Midlands, moult on the Beauly Firth.

BEWICK'S SWAN

This species does not need to be ringed to be individually identifiable. Detailed observations, started at the Wildfowl Trust headquarters at Slimbridge by Sir Peter Scott and continued by a succession of research workers, have shown that the pattern of black and yellow on each bird's bill is as unique as a human's fingerprints. The birds wintering there have now been logged in and out over more than twenty years.

There has also been a colour ringing programme, using large rings engraved with a code, to enable those not privy to the secrets of bill pattern identification to keep track of the birds away from Slimbridge. The birds are now regularly spotted at various points on their

Bewick's Swans breed on arctic tundra.

migration from the breeding grounds in northern Russia to Gloucestershire. Each winter there are dozens of sightings from the flocks of Bewick's Swans in the Netherlands.

REDWINGS

These attractive small thrushes are one of the most distinctive and widespread of our winter migrants. They move westwards from the central and eastern parts of northern Europe to spend the winter in the warmer areas, where the Gulf Stream influences the weather. They have a very distinctive thin squeak used as a contact call and can be heard, particularly on misty nights, passing westwards during October and November.

Ringing recoveries show that the same birds that wintered in Britain, France or Iberia in one winter (often their first) may be found in later winters far to the East. Ringing recoveries have come particularly from Trans-Caspia (Georgia), Turkey and Greece and even Iran.

Many Redwing move on when snow comes.

These appear to be birds from populations deep in the Soviet Union which alter their wintering site from year to year.

BRAMBLING

This finch is a close relative of the Chaffinch and it often appears in mixed flocks. Its presence is spasmodic and there are, from time to time, immense flocks feeding in areas where the beech trees have had a good crop of mast. Some roosts have been estimated to contain more than 50 000 000 birds at a time. In parts of Germany, a few years ago, so many birds spent the winter that the public had to be reassured that there was nothing for people to worry about when they blocked out the sun.

Like most migrant finches, Brambling are not just nocturnal migrants but are also regularly seen moving by day. They are easiest seen on the move along the East Coast, as they arrive, or where the

Seeds can be difficult to find under snow.

migrating birds follow a guiding line, such as a river valley or line of hills.

STARLING

It comes as a surprise to many people to discover that such common birds as the Starling and Blackbird are actually migrants. In fact the British breeding populations are fairly sedentary but are joined by millions of other birds during the winter. They are driven out of their Continental breeding areas by the cold weather and are completely absent, during the winter, from such places as Finland

and Poland. Indeed the Starling is looked upon in much the same way as we greet Swallows, the harbinger of spring.

The Starlings which come to us swell the population to such an extent that the species is undoubtedly our commonest bird during the winter. The roosts that they form are a spectacular feature of the winter's birding. Some may contain more than a million birds. As they move out from it in the early morning, in all directions, they can be seen on radar screens as radiating circles – just like the ripples when a pebble is thrown into a pond.

LESSER WHITETHROAT

This little warbler is one of the few species of summer migrants from Britain that moves to the south-east and winters in East Africa and not West Africa. This is because they were confined to the eastern end of the Mediterranean during the last glaciation and the population has spread to the north and west as the ice receded.

Ringing recoveries show that the foothills of the Alps, in northern Italy, were used by the migrants on their way southwards to fatten up. However, there has only been one recent recovery from this area and it may be that they are now going directly to the Nile Delta area. They then have to put on weight to reach the wintering area in Ethiopia. On the return journey in spring the fattening area is in Asia Minor, and Lesser Whitethroats have been recovered in Israel, Lebanon, Syria and Cyprus.

The Lesser Whitethroat winters in East Africa.

WHITETHROAT

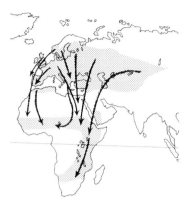

This used to be almost as common a summer migrant as the Willow Warbler. However, it migrates south-west to winter in the Sahel zone just south of the Sahara. Like many other species it migrates first to north-west Spain and then, after fattening, makes a non-stop flight to the wintering area.

Unfortunately when drought in the Sahel began to bite, the effect on the Whitethroat population was immediate and dramatic. Over the winter of 1968–69, more than two-thirds of the birds we expected to come back failed to return. Since then the population has fluctuated and actually declined a little further. Some other Sahel wintering species, including the Sedge Warbler and Redstart, were also affected.

The Common Whitethroat winters just south of the Sahara.

WRYNECK

This primitive woodpecker is a long-distance migrant and used to be a familiar bird in Britain some fifty years ago. Very few now breed in Britain, but it is not uncommon on migration in the autumn. These are birds from the Scandinavian breeding population which are on their way to the south-south-west and Iberia to put on weight for their final migration to West Africa.

They are particularly characteristic visitors along the East Coast, when there is poor weather with south-easterly winds. They may then appear, with other Scandinavian migrants like Icterine Warblers, Redstarts, Pied Flycatchers, Whinchats and Barred Warblers, in some numbers at such sites as Spurn Point on the Humber or Cley on the bulge of Norfolk.

In a few classic years, literally thousands of birds have made their landfall together and even brought the traffic to a halt in some resorts. This happens when migration has been held up for some time and the birds have 'jumped the gun' and set out in large numbers only to find that the conditions were not good enough for them to continue successfully.

The Wryneck is superbly camouflaged.

WREN

One hardly thinks of the Wren as a migrant, but considerable numbers of British Wrens do migrate over short distances. Indeed a very few actually make it to the south coast of France. However, examination of the recoveries and intensive catching at various sites in southern England has shown a distinct switch in the areas they are using.

The birds are not able to breed successfully in really wet habitats, like reed beds, for their low nest would be very likely to be swamped if there was a lot of rain. Such habitats are ideal for them in the winter, and some ringers regularly catch several dozen Wrens a day in reed-bed habitats. On the other hand some rather high Chiltern woodlands, with good undergrowth, have very dense breeding populations of Wrens. However, these all leave during the winter when the vegetation dies down and the woods become too cold and exposed for them. The fact that the birds have only moved very short distances does not mean they have not migrated.

BIRD OBSERVATORIES

Scattered round our coasts are roughly a dozen establishments where migrants are regularly watched, counted and ringed. This is the bird observatory network and they range from the purpose-built hostel on Fair Isle, halfway between the Shetlands and Orkneys, to little huts manned on a voluntary basis by local enthusiasts.

Most observatories welcome visitors and several are on romantic island sites (Fair Isle, North Ronaldsay, Isle of May, Bardsey, Calf of Man, Copeland and Cape Clear). Others are rather easier to reach (Spurn, Gibraltar Point, Landguard, Sandwich Bay, Dungeness, Portland Bill and Walney) as they are actually on the mainland. A list of those that are open during the current year is available from the BTO Ringing Office.

Whilst the observatories are mainly aimed at watching migration, all sorts of other activities take place there. These include general natural history courses, working parties and also detailed research on local bird populations. In particular, very detailed work is being carried out at Fair Isle on the exceptionally rich seabird colonies of the island.

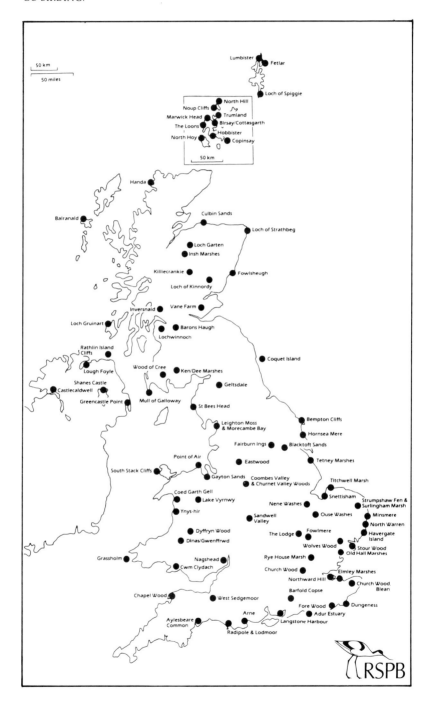

50 km

50 miles

Lumbister
Fetlar
Loch of Spiggie
North Hill
Noup Cliffs
Trumland
Marwick Head
Birsay/Cottasgarth
The Loons
Hobbister
North Hoy
Copinsay
50 km

Handa

Balranald

Culbin Sands
Loch of Strathbeg
Loch Garten
Insh Marshes
Killiecrankie
Fowlsheugh
Loch of Kinnordy
Inversnaid
Vane Farm
Loch Gruinart
Barons Haugh
Lochwinnoch
Rathlin Island Cliffs
Lough Foyle
Wood of Cree
Ken/Dee Marshes
Coquet Island
Shanes Castle
Castlecaldwell
Geltsdale
Greencastle Point
Mull of Galloway
St Bees Head
Bempton Cliffs
Leighton Moss & Morecambe Bay
Hornsea Mere
Fairburn Ings
Blacktoft Sands
Point of Air
Eastwood
Tetney Marshes
South Stack Cliffs
Gayton Sands
Coombes Valley & Churnet Valley Woods
Titchwell Marsh
Coed Garth Gell
Snettisham
Lake Vyrnwy
Nene Washes
Strumpshaw Fen & Surlingham Marsh
Ynys-hir
Ouse Washes
Minsmere
Sandwell Valley
North Warren
Dyffryn Wood
The Lodge
Fowlmere
Havergate Island
Dinas/Gwenffrwd
Wolves Wood
Stour Wood
Grassholm
Rye House Marsh
Old Hall Marshes
Nagshead
Church Wood
Elmley Marshes
Cwm Clydach
Northward Hill
Church Wood Blean
Chapel Wood
Barfold Copse
West Sedgemoor
Fore Wood
Dungeness
Arne
Adur Estuary
Aylesbeare Common
Langstone Harbour
Radipole & Lodmoor

RSPB

6

BIRD MANAGEMENT

Bob Scott

Interest in wildlife and conservation, particularly birds, has grown steadily from the 1950s and 1960s until the present day. Compare membership of an organisation such as the Royal Society for the Protection of Birds, which had 10500 members in 1960, with today's figure of some 500000. Coupled with this, there has been a growing awareness that many of the scarce or threatened areas of Britain can only be safeguarded by declaring them reserves or protected areas.

Organisations devoted to the study and protection of wildlife have started to thrive. The network of county wildlife or nature conservation trusts has grown until every county is represented. The Woodland Trust has devoted its energies to saving wooded sites throughout Britain, and the RSPB has developed a network of national reserves that expanded from some seven sites, covering 1290 hectares (3200 acres), in 1950 to the present total of more than 120 reserves covering over 57000 hectares (141000 acres).

The historical concept of a nature reserve was an area that was fenced and protected. It was available for the wildlife, and even people were not always allowed entrance to an area that they, either directly or indirectly, had made possible. During the 1960s and 1970s this situation changed, and changed very dramatically. The pressures on the countryside in a crowded country such as Britain were great. The demand for recreational facilities also increased as the population became more affluent. Birdwatching became a rapidly expanding hobby and the associated industry followed behind. The demand for optical equipment grew and specialist dealers in binoculars, telescopes and cameras blossomed. Organised birdwatching holidays and tours flourished and a new bird book was being published at a rate of more than one per week.

An increasing demand to visit sites and see birds that were being protected in special areas led to more visitor facilities on nature reserves. Car parks and nature trails, toilet blocks, information centres and shops became a feature of the more popular sites, and people came to realise that the very habitats that made these sites so special needed work to maintain them. From there it was a relatively short step to carrying out work to create a new habitat. The land was being managed to maximise its wildlife productivity just as farmland is managed to maximise its food productivity.

Nature reserves still occupy a very small proportion of the total land surface of Britain (less than 8%), but it is clear that a diversity of habitat within a reserve, if not detrimental to other interests, is one way of ensuring maximum value for each site.

All habitats or ecosystems are dynamic and constantly changing. Some, such as an oak wood, may take nearly 400 years to develop full maturity. Others can show changes more dramatically: reed beds can quickly dry out as leaf-litter from each year's growth accumulates and provides a suitable material for the first invading sallow bushes and the site becomes dominated by willow carr. Heathlands can quickly loose their stands of heather as encroaching pine becomes dominant and the site becomes a coniferous woodland.

Not all ecosystems or bird species lend themselves to protection via a system of nature reserves. The Golden Eagle requires such a vast area of upland terrain that, apart from protecting its nest, it would not be possible to safeguard the species by declaring a nature reserve. Hedgerow species depend for their survival on the attitude of landowners throughout Britain, and setting up a hedgerow reserve would do little to improve protection.

It is the specialised sites where reserves come into their own – the reed beds, heathlands, flooded grazing marshes, intertidal estuaries and selected woodlands such as Caledonian pine forests or oaks on Welsh hillsides. The RSPB now employs a network of wardens. It is their job to blend together all the different facets that form part of a reserve operation – the protection and study of the wildlife present, the maintenance and management of the site, and ensuring that the activities of visitors do not conflict with the interests of the local community.

Over the years the RSPB has developed skills and knowledge on the active management of a wide range of habitats. This provides an unrivalled source of data that is slowly being assembled and documented.

Each reserve is assessed and carefully studied. From this, a management plan is developed and this points the way forward for future development. Management plans are fluid working documents, constantly assessed, changed and amended in the light of additional knowledge. Every year further monitoring of bird populations, studies of the vegetation or the flow and quality of the water supply will indicate potential problems or possibilities for improvements. Just what are the specific food requirements of a particular bird species? Why has the phosphate content of the water supply increased? What is the importance of the reserve for flowering plants, butterflies, beetles, etc?

RSPB RESERVES

The following are just some of the numerous examples of management undertaken on RSPB reserves.

Havergate Island, Suffolk

This 108-hectare (267-acre) island near the mouth of the river Alde is reached from the quay at Orford. It forms part of the Orfordness National Nature Reserve, and the long shingle spit of Orfordness protects the river and Havergate Island from the North Sea. The island attained ornithological fame in 1947 when it became the site for the recolonisation of Britain by breeding Avocets. Avocets had ceased to nest in Britain by the end of the nineteenth century, but the reason for their decline and eventual disappearance remains a mystery. As always in these cases there is probably a combination of factors involved but from a widespread population, stretching from Humberside in the north to the Kent/Sussex border in the south, the numbers steadily decreased.

As a defence measure against possible invasion in the Second World War, previously drained areas of east coast marshes were

Avocets re-colonised Britain on habitat created and managed by man.

flooded. This provided the habitat and undisturbed areas necessary for Avocet recolonisation to take place. The Havergate population steadily increased from four pairs in 1947 to one hundred pairs in 1968. In 1949, the RSPB committed itself to protecting this nucleus of recolonisation by buying the island, installing a warden and maintaining a regular watch over the infant colony.

One duty of the wardening staff on all reserves is to monitor the bird populations and their changing fortunes, and it was this regular monitoring that was to indicate a problem facing the Avocets – suddenly their productivity was decreasing. From some 100 pairs rearing 178 young in 1969, a similar number only reared 12 young in 1976. Something was clearly wrong and a study was implemented to discover why the productivity had fallen and what was necessary to correct the situation. If no action were taken, the Avocet would once again be lost as a breeding species, for no population can survive with such limited recruitment to its numbers.

The first indications were that the Avocets were hatching their eggs satisfactorily, but it was during fledging that the mortality was occurring. The chicks were dying on the island. A close examination of the food supply and salinity of the water on the island provided the answer. Avocets feed on a range of small invertebrates that live in slightly saline water, such as the estuarine shrimp. These animals cannot live in sea water, but require a mixture of both salt and fresh water. One would expect to find such water in a river mouth and associated marshes where sea and river water mix. The problem on Havergate Island was that the flooded areas were acting as salt pans. Each year water would evaporate from these areas, leaving behind salt, and the salinity levels were thus increasing. Only if a particularly wet season produced sufficient rain water to dilute the salt was there a good food supply. The answer was to undertake a management programme that would enable the salt content of the island to be controlled.

It was decided that the solution lay in 'flushing' the island clean of excess salt whenever necessary. To achieve this a major sluice was constructed in the sea wall, allowing river water to flow into and across the island and exit at a sluice near the other end of the island. Each year there are regular measurements of the island's salinity, and careful checks on the Avocet population and its productivity. Following the work in 1985, the breeding population of 123 pairs produced 122 young – a clear indication of success.

As with so many management programmes aimed principally at one particular species, there was a dramatic spin-off. The improved food supply undoubtedly assisted the Avocets, but other species also exploited the improvement. Havergate Island is a regular stopping point for many waders migrating between their northern breeding grounds and their wintering quarters further south in Europe or Africa. The abundant food supply enables both waders and wintering wildfowl to feed on the island.

Elmley Marshes, Kent

On the southern shore of the Isle of Sheppey and overlooking the estuary of the river Swale, Elmley Marshes form part of the famous North Kent Marshes that have justifiably earned a place in ornithological record books. Here the rivers Thames, Medway and Swale pass through an area of low-lying land that, in the past, was notorious for its swamps and tidal flats. As the rich pastures were established and turned over to agriculture, large areas were reclaimed from the sea and drained to prevent flooding. In the early 1970s, the RSPB made a concentrated effort to establish a reserve in the area to combat the continued pattern of drainage and embanking that was so destructive to wildlife. After a careful examination of the ground and discussions with the owners, the RSPB leased the site from a charity, the Oxford University Chest. At that time the reserve consisted of low-lying embanked land that excluded all tidal water and was carefully ditched and sluiced to facilitate the removal of any surface water. There was good, but dry grazing land which lacked the wildfowl and waders that had inhabited the site in their thousands in the past. The challenge was to bring them back.

The first key was water, water in sufficient quantity and under sufficient control to maintain a flood without damaging neighbouring farmland. The second key was for cattle to graze the grass in just the correct manner to provide the important structure of tussocks for breeding birds, and short cropped patches for grazing birds such as geese and wigeon. Here was an opportunity to show that farming and bird reserve management could work side by side.

First of all, some of the natural drainage channels had to be blocked. The winter rains flooded a section of grassland, and the birds responded next spring with a marked increase in breeding numbers. Redshanks, in particular, leapt from eleven to sixty pairs! As the summer progressed, however, the flood dried and the ground cracked. A guaranteed source of water was necessary. Consultations with the water authority led to some major changes in the flow system and the RSPB was granted permission to impound water. Elmley Fleet, the main drainage channel through the reserve, was dammed in order to create a large reservoir capable of holding some five million gallons of water. This was enough to maintain the

The management of Elmley reserve has increased the wintering population of Wigeon to peaks of more than 20,000 birds.

flooded area through two dry years. It was now possible to recreate the wetland reserve that had been the intention from the start.

It is very easy for the visitor to look at Elmley now and not fully realise the work that has been necessary. Observation hides have obviously been constructed, the car park and toilet block have been built – but surely the flocks of ducks and waders feeding or resting beside the pools of water have always been there? We must not forget the countless hours of hard work contributed by volunteers from the RSPB and other organisations. These same volunteers made it possible to mechanise the work, for the heavy earth-moving equipment costs money and it is the supporters of conservation and reserve operations that provide the resources. A visit to Elmley today is very different from a visit in the mid-1970s. Only some 180 visitors saw the reserve in 1978 when visiting began, but in 1986 there were over 8000.

The success of the Elmley Marshes flooding programme demonstrates just how rich the bird life must have been in the past – for here, within the 13 000 hectares (32 000 acres) of the North Kent Marshes, is some 280 hectares (700 acres) that not only holds a vast variety of wintering and breeding birds, but also provides a secure and undisturbed site for the huge numbers of waders that gather when the high tide forces them from the rich feeding grounds of the estuarine mud.

Additions to the reserve's breeding list have included Black-tailed Godwit, Avocet and Pintail and more than ten established breeding species have shown dramatic increases. Wintering populations have increased; a 'modest' 3000 Wigeon before management now number in excess of 20 000; 1500 Lapwing number 17 000.

Once again the work has provided unexpected 'spin-offs'. The number of birds and species that use the reserve makes Elmley a site of international importance. As a consequence it is now twinned with ornithological sites elsewhere in Europe so that information and expertise can be exchanged. The concentrations of birds, including such species as Yellow Wagtail (up to forty-eight breeding pairs) and Skylark (over 450 pairs) now regularly attract predators such as Peregrines, Merlins and Short-eared Owls. Up to forty Herons regularly feed at the site, visitors from the other RSPB North Kent reserve at Northward Hill, which houses Britain's largest heronry of some 200 pairs.

Arne, Dorset

The heathlands of southern England have faced a period of steady and quite dramatic loss. Conversion for agriculture, reclamation for forestry or simply change to development for housing or industry have had an effect on expanses of heaths from Surrey and Sussex westward to Devon. Only in areas where the military have controlled the land or within the great heathlands of the New Forest has there been any form of protection – but even here over-grazing and repeated fires have destroyed the important character of this now seriously threatened ecosystem. Some 22 500 hectares (56 000 acres) of heathlands in Dorset and west Hampshire in the late 1800s is now reduced to less than 5 600 hectares (14 000 acres), of which a considerable proportion is still threatened with development in one form or another.

Amongst one of the largest remaining blocks is the RSPB reserve at Arne, situated on the peninsula that bears its name and protruding into the north-west corner of Poole harbour. From the high ground of Shipstal Point on the reserve's nature trail, there are views across the open water of the harbour to the contrasting coastline of urban Poole and Parkstone as well as to the more isolated area of the National Trust site of Brownsea Island. Arne forms part of the Purbeck heathlands, but when the site was acquired as a reserve in 1965 it was quite obvious that much of the heath had already been lost, although remnants were clearly visible amongst the steadily encroaching pines, gorse and bracken.

The variety of wildlife that inhabits heathland is, by contrast with many areas, somewhat impoverished. What it lacks in variety, however, is more than compensated for by the uniqueness of the species that do exist. The bird speciality is, without question, the Dartford Warbler, a small whitethroat-like warbler that, together with the Cetti's Warbler which is also concentrated in Dorset and the south-west, can claim fame as a resident British warbler. All other British breeding warblers migrate southwards each winter to escape the severity of the weather. The numbers of Dartford Warblers present on Arne each year varies in response to the temperature, and more importantly the snowfall, during the preceding winter. The other bird inhabitants of Arne heath mainly desert the area each winter. The Tree Pipits, Stonechats, Yellowhammers and Nightjars all move away and the heath becomes a quiet place with its few Dart-

In severe winter weather, with heavy snow, the survival of Dartford Warblers is dependent upon the shelter provided by clumps of gorse.

ford Warblers and the surprisingly hardy Wrens. At this time of year wintering Hen Harriers and Short-eared Owls may move in to feed on the voles in years of abundance.

Birds, however, are just one feature of this fragile habitat. Specialist plant species share the ground with the heathers, and in the wet boggy depressions sundew and bog asphodel are mixed amongst the carpet of *Sphagnum* moss. Sand lizard and smooth snake share the site with the other four species of British reptiles and an amazing richness of insect life includes some twenty-two species of dragonflies.

The management programme for the Arne reserve was to maintain and improve the quality of the existing heath, while at the same time re-establishing new heath from the areas that had been lost. The task was formidable, and was inevitably labour-intensive. This was not a job that could be tackled by machine, for heavy machinery on the heathlands would destroy the very fragile structure of the habitat that it was intended to safeguard.

The existing heath needs two major features: a diversity of age structure amongst the heather, and small clumps of healthy gorse bushes that would provide that all important shelter for the Dartford Warblers in winters with high snowfall. The age structure is achieved by a programme of mowing or, where necessary, a very carefully controlled system of burning. Ironically fire can be heathlands' saving and also its greatest threat. The very dryness of the habitat means that an uncontrolled fire can sweep through vast areas in a matter of hours, destroying years of careful work. A system of firebreaks has to be installed to prevent such a catastrophe. The gorse clumps can be established by digging small sand banks upon which seedling gorse bushes are planted. Like all heathland plants on the poor soils, they are slow-growing; but as they develop, the exposed sandy banks are used as breeding grounds by the reserve's reptiles.

If maintaining the existing heath requires manpower, then re-establishing lost heath requires even more. Two species invade the Arne reserve with apparent ease – the Scots pine and the rhododendron. Over the years, many acres of heathland have been lost, but slowly the situation is being changed. The cleared pine can perhaps be sold as pulp or firewood, which brings some small income, but the rhododendron is simply stacked and burnt. The stumps of the pine die in the ground, but the rhododendron must be killed or the sprouting shoots threaten to undo the work done. The task does not end here, for all too often the ground cleared ready for the recolonising heather that has laid dormant for many years is covered with invading bracken. A dense cover of bracken will prevent heather becoming established as effectively as the pine and rhododendron that was removed. Yet another programme is then implemented to remove the bracken by means of a highly specific spray. Then, and only then, will the heather return to its former glory.

The gorse clumps amongst the heather must be maintained in a healthy condition. If left they eventually become old and 'leggy', no longer serving the purpose of a winter safeguard for the Dartford Warbler. The gorse clumps must be cut in rotation to ensure that healthy vigorous growth is always present. As with all habitat management, the work never comes to an end; the very maintenance of the ecosystem is a work programme in itself.

Fowlmere, Cambridgeshire

In 1977 the Young Ornithologists' Club, the junior branch of the RSPB, raised enough money to buy the reserve at Fowlmere near Cambridge. This 35-hectare (86-acre) site forms a unique oasis in an otherwise arable desert. Surrounded by open fields, mainly used for cereal crops and lacking in hedges or other features to break the monotony of the landscape, Fowlmere with its reed beds, thorn scrub and disused watercress beds attracts many birds.

A thriving Reed Warbler population requires healthy reeds and a good
food supply, both achieved by correct water management.

Breeding birds include a large population of Reed and Sedge
Warblers nesting in the edges of the reed beds and feeding in the surrounding scrub, Kingfishers beside the river and Water Rails in the
dense vegetation. Each spring the reserve plays host to a wide
variety of summer migrants, including several warblers such as
Grasshopper Warbler and Lesser Whitethroat. Turtle Doves are
common and Cuckoos lay their eggs in the nests of Reed Warblers
and Dunnocks.

Winter brings its own attractions to Fowlmere. The surrounding
farmland can provide food for a range of thrush and finch species;
Fowlmere, with its dense clumps of hawthorn, can provide secure
overnight roosting sites. A spectacular sight on a January evening, in
the failing light, is the steady arrival of several species. Redwings
and Fieldfares dominate the thrushes, with large flocks of Corn Buntings and Pied Wagtails outnumbering the other finches. Even an occasional Hen Harrier or two will use the site.

The management plan for Fowlmere stated that not only was the
habitat to be improved for birds, but this was to be done in such a
way that visitors, particularly children, could appreciate the site and
see many of the species. Fowlmere has no permanent warden, only
seasonal contract staff, and as such was very dependent upon volunteers. Fortunately Cambridge has many very keen supporters of the
RSPB including a thriving members group, and with their assistance
the jobs could be tackled.

First there was the visitor facilities. A nature trail was relatively easy to lay out, although where it passed through some of the wettest parts of the reserve a certain amount of board walk had to be constructed. A slight diversion led down to a small, newly excavated pond where dipping with nets provided great educational potential. The countless frogs and toads that colonised the new pond obviously approved! Another addition to the trail provided a pathway accessible to wheelchairs, enabling visitors who would not normally be able to tour the reserve to gain access to a quiet secluded spot among the reeds.

Observation hides were high on the agenda, and the first was an ambitious structure. The plan was to construct a hide with views all round, large enough to seat a complete coach party of children and raised some 15 feet into the air to give an excellent view across the reserve. The local volunteers tackled the task with relish, even if it did mean several weekends of hard, muddy work. The foundations had to be dug, the uprights set in concrete, and the hide built upon the platform. All the materials had to be manhandled along a mile or more of muddy, chalky, slippery roadway. Finally the task was complete, the hide in position and ready for use. How many of the subsequent visitors appreciated the hours of hard work that went into the construction? They certainly appreciated the excellent views that became possible. Swallows nested underneath the hide, Reed Warblers collecting food amongst the bushes actually flew through the hide and out of the viewing slots back to their nests with young in the reeds. An extensive water area immediately in front of the hide was colonised by Little Grebes and Tufted Duck. The raised water level in the reed bed encouraged Bearded Tits to stay and nest, while each summer the lucky birdwatcher is treated to a Hobby hawking dragonflies over the pool.

A further hide has now been added and the reserve has been extended. New facilities, including a car park and additional nature trails, are planned. For the wildlife, careful consideration is now being given to further improvements and ways of maintaining the existing importance. In common with many RSPB reserves, Fowlmere is a Site of Special Scientific Interest and contains much of ecological importance in addition to its bird life. The RSPB consults closely with the Nature Conservancy Council on all activities.

Minsmere, Suffolk

Minsmere can perhaps justifiably claim to be the best-known bird reserve in Britain. Indeed, its fame has spread throughout the world. Situated on the Suffolk coastline between Southwold and Aldeburgh, Minsmere is now somewhat dominated by the Sizewell nuclear power station to the south. Changes, however, are not new to the Minsmere scene. In the late 1800s the natural marshes and mere were lost through drainage and the site of the present reserve was devoted to agriculture. In 1940 the reserve was re-flooded as a wartime defence measure. The dramatic results of this flooding, including the nesting by Avocets, encouraged the RSPB to lease the site from Captain A. Ogilvie who then owned it. The 595-hectare (1470-acre) reserve was announced in 1947; in the 1970s, following a 'Save a Place for Birds' appeal, the RSPB raised sufficient funds to purchase the area. Since that time Minsmere has received many accolades, culminating with the awarding in 1979 of the Council for Europe's Diploma for a protected area of European interest.

The story of changes and developments at Minsmere makes fascinating reading, but it is perhaps the creation of what was to become known as the 'Scrape' that was the most exciting project ever undertaken on a RSPB reserve at that time.

The construction of the 'Scrape' consisted of several distinct stages. Bulldozers prepared the basic area, taking off the surface material and using the resulting spoil to prepare rough islands and embankments to hold water. A nearby area was banked up to hold sufficient fresh water to feed the site and achieve the correct mix with sea water to maintain salinity at the right level. The system is now operated via a series of sluices and dams, through which adjustable plastic piping can be set at any required height to ensure the greatest amount of automatic control possible. Salt water can be obtained at high tide via a main sluice to the sea.

The nesting, feeding and roosting islands within the scrape were constructed in different shapes, sizes and surfaces. This made it possible to attract a wide variety of bird species. Although the basic island construction was carried out by machine, all needed a considerable amount of 'hand' work to finish them off. The edges of each island had to shelve gradually, to ensure that they were suitable for both adults and unfledged young. The surfaces ranged from mud to stone: layers of polythene sacks were placed on the surface of the islands and then covered by whatever material (stone, sand or even mussel shells) was required. Carrying materials to the islands often involved building temporary tracks capable of taking the weight of a tractor and trailer, but even so the task facing the wardens, both staff and volunteers, was daunting. For one island alone, 3000 polythene sacks and 100 tons of gravel were required. The gravel had to be transported in loads of 1½ tons each and then spread by hand across the surface of the island. It was well worth all the hard work, however, for Avocets began to nest on the new area in 1963.

Twenty-five years later, the work is still continuing. The original 'Scrape' has been extended, resulting in a most successful Little Tern colony, and somewhat surprisingly, the colony of Avocets moved into the newly created area in preference to their previous sites.

The many changes at Minsmere over the years are reflected in the changes to the bird population and the interest shown by visitors. In 1949 there were some 85 species breeding on the reserve, a further 60 or so were recorded and some 47 visitors enjoyed a day at the reserve. By contrast, some 100 species now nest on the reserve, over 200 species are recorded in most years and the annual visitor total is in the region of 40000.

Leighton Moss, Lancashire

Leighton Moss lies close to the coastline at Morecambe Bay. At one time the site was tidal, but now it is separated from the sea by an embankment and sluice which keeps the Moss filled with fresh water. As a consequence it contains an abundant growth of reeds. Leighton is unique in many ways. It is one of the most north-westerly reed beds in Britain and as such contains several species on the very edge of their breeding distribution, including Reed Warbler and Bearded Tit. It is one of the few sites in England where a visitor could reasonably expect to see otters and also the rare Bittern. Bitterns have decreased dramatically as a breeding species in Britain, the total population now numbering less than thirty pairs. Of these, up to thirteen nest annually at Leighton.

A feature at Leighton has been the establishment of visitor facilities. A large barn has been converted into an extensive information centre complete with displays, art exhibition, shop and information room. Out on the reserve itself is a network of public visiting areas

Leighton Moss reserve
LEFT Warden harvesting reeds
BELOW Building a hide

plus sites for permit holders and members only. Four observation hides give views across the lagoons and reed beds, and it is from these that the visitor can expect to see otters and Bitterns.

Reserve management for Bitterns followed a careful programme of study into the species' requirements. Detailed observations and recording of the birds' behaviour, both at Leighton Moss and other nesting sites, were undertaken over a number of years. Sites where the males were 'booming' or calling were carefully mapped and flight paths across the reeds were faithfully recorded. Very slowly a pattern of behaviour and requirements was established. It became apparent that the balance between reed beds and areas of open water was critical to the Bitterns' needs. The birds bred within the dense reed where the nests could be well secluded and undisturbed, but for feeding they needed to walk out from the reeds and into open water. A close examination clearly showed that where extensive areas of reeds contained no water, the Bittern population was low. Areas of reed divided by open water could support more breeding pairs. Indeed the flight paths recorded from the observations showed that Bitterns nesting in extensive reed beds needed to fly to open water to feed and obtain food for their young. Where water was close at hand such long journeys were not necessary, and nests were closer together.

In the days when Leighton Moss had been drained for agriculture, the system supported a network of drainage ditches. Aerial photographs indicated that even though the site was now flooded and covered with a growth of reed, the old ditches could still be seen. It was planned to open up these ditches within the reed bed, keeping the ends firmly blocked off, and convert them into linear ponds throughout the reeds, providing a new feeding area for nesting Bitterns. Reed bed is fragile habitat and the introduction of machinery to excavate a ditch system could do more harm than good. The reed bed was also very wet and there was a definite danger of machinery becoming bogged down. Fortunately there exists a machine called an 'aquacat', a small digger that actually floats as it works. As the ditch is dug out, the 'aquacat' floats along its own creation. The ditch line was marked on the ground by volunteers wading through head-high reeds and positioning tall poles that the 'aquacat' driver could follow. The resulting ditches, invisible from the ground, provided the feeding grounds necessary; and although the increase in the Bittern population from 8–10 pairs to 11–13 pairs seems small, it is significant in relation to the total British population.

Yet again the story does not end neatly. If the ditches were left, they would quickly be covered by a fresh growth of reeds; and for them to achieve their object it is necessary to maintain them as open water. Every year one side of the ditch is hand-cut to prevent reed encroachment. This means that there is always reed growth close to the water to enable the Bittern to walk into its feeding area but never enough growth to choke the open water. Once again, the operation is made possible by the many voluntary workers on the reserve.

Titchwell Marsh, Norfolk

The north Norfolk coast is probably one of the best protected coastlines in the British Isles. A series of nature reserves extends from near King's Lynn almost to Cromer. Amongst these, at the village of Titchwell, is the RSPB Titchwell Marsh reserve, acquired in 1973 when the site was almost exclusively saltmarsh vegetation that was completely covered by the high spring tides. On the inland edge was a poor quality reed bed where fresh water flowed into the marsh.

Over a period of some ten years, dramatic changes became possible. These changes not only affected the very nature of the habitat but also produced striking increases in bird populations and provided excellent opportunities for visiting birdwatchers to see them. The key to the work centred around the construction of sea walls, intended to keep the regular tides off the land and enable a controlled water system to be operated. Both fresh and salt water were available, so banks and pipes in the right places enabled total control. A walk along the visitor route to the sea at Titchwell today shows just what a change has taken place. To the west is an area of saltmarsh, much as all Titchwell was in the past; to the east are the managed areas of the reserve. Travelling northwards from the visitor centre towards the sea, the first habitat to be encountered is reed bed. In this totally fresh water, the reed has developed strong and healthy plants supporting breeding populations of Bittern, Bearded Tit and Marsh Harrier. Further spread of the reed into the next section, open fresh water marsh, is prevented by a deep ditch. Reeds spread by rhizomes and will not grow when the water is too deep. An embankment separates the two areas so that water levels in each can be controlled independently.

The next area is fresh water marsh. High water levels in the winter make this an attractive site for dabbling ducks, such as Shoveler, Teal and Pintail. At the same time the flood water prevents the establishment of vegetation on the mud and islands, which later in the year are important for migrant and breeding birds. The water flowing through the reed bed provides the reservoir should it be needed. When not, it is diverted around the fresh water marsh and out to sea.

The next embankment separates the fresh water marsh from a saline water marsh. This contains a mixture of salt and fresh water in carefully measured quantities so as to provide ideal feeding and nesting areas for, in particular, the Avocet population that has recently colonised the site. Once again the water levels in this marsh can be controlled in isolation from the rest of the reserve, so that levels can be dropped to provide suitable feeding and yet raised when necessary to provide secure nesting sites.

The final embankment leads to the original salt marsh, still open to the sea and subject to regular flooding on the high spring tides.

Ten years of careful planning and extensive work have led to a massive increase in bird populations. Thirty-nine breeding species in 1973 had increased to sixty-one in 1982. Twenty-six of these nesting species had shown an increase over the preceding ten years, and forty-five non-breeding species also increased in numbers or frequency of visits.

Management work on RSPB reserves is a carefully planned and researched programme aimed at enhancing the bird populations without damaging other wildlife in the area. It is dependent upon the skills and dedication of the professional staff that work on the reserves, but would be impossible without the countless hours of enthusiasm from the hundreds of volunteers who give up their holidays and weekends to work on the reserves. Even their task would not be possible without the hundreds of thousands of RSPB supporters who provide funds through their membership fees and money-raising efforts. Conservation and reserve management in Britain is fortunate to operate within an atmosphere of public sympathy and support that makes so much possible.

APPENDICES

I

SOCIETIES

BRITISH TRUST FOR ORNITHOLOGY (BTO)
Beech Grove, Tring, Hertfordshire HP23 5NR

The British Trust for Ornithology (BTO) is dedicated to the study and appreciation of birds through a programme of long and short-term surveys. More than eight thousand members nationwide help to map the summer and winter distributions of birds, trace migration patterns and investigate bird breeding biology. Other surveys identify habitats and sites vital to bird conservation and study the potential effects of new environmental developments. With its computerised data banks, representing over fifty years of research, the BTO is the envy of the ornithological world.

The current major BTO project, the *New Atlas of Breeding Birds in Britain and Ireland*, aims to map the distribution of every species of wild bird in Britain. The results will be published in 1991 and will include information on the overall numbers of birds, habitats, and the effects of land use on bird populations. Details of the Atlas project and how to take part can be obtained from the address above.

The Trust is also involved in setting up a National Centre for Ornithology – the first of its kind in the world. Some six acres have been given for the Centre, in Tring, Hertfordshire, by the Hon. Jacob Rothschild and the Trustees of the British Museum, and the project is expected to be completed by the end of 1991. An appeal for £1.5 million to build the Centre is under way.

The BTO offers its members a regular bulletin, *BTO News*, the option of subscribing to its own journals, *Bird Study* and *Ringing & Migration*, a chance to participate in its surveys, a network of regional representatives, national and regional birdwatchers' conferences, training courses in census techniques, and advice and information from the Trust's staff.

The BTO has members from all walks of life. Whether you are a back garden birdwatcher, a keen amateur fieldworker or a professional ornithologist there is a place for you in the BTO. The basic yearly subscription is £12.00, while fellowship, which includes *Bird Study*, costs £17.50. Concessionary rates for OAPs and students are also available. If you would like to know more about membership of the BTO please write for details, enclosing a large stamped addressed envelope, to the Membership Secretary, BTO, Beech Grove, Tring, Herts HP23 5NR.

ROYAL SOCIETY FOR THE PROTECTION OF BIRDS (RSPB)
The Lodge, Sandy, Bedfordshire SG19 2DL

The RSPB is a registered charity dependent on the voluntary support of its members. Founded in 1889 and incorporated under Royal Charter in 1904, it is Europe's largest and most forward-looking conservation organisation and has over 400 000 members. It owns or leases over 115 reserves covering more than 140 000 acres, most of which are open to members free of charge, and has a national network of regional offices. It also runs the Young Ornithologists' Club for young people aged 16 and under.

The Society undertakes research into the many problems facing wild birds today and, in investigating the effects of environmental change on bird populations, acts as an advisory body to government and industry. In this, it co-operates with other national and international conservation organisations, both in the UK and abroad. The RSPB aims to inform people about birds through a wide range of films, publications, lectures, exhibitions and talks, and also publicises and helps to enforce the bird protection laws.

Members of the RSPB receive a full colour magazine, *Birds*, four times a year, and are eligible to join the countrywide network of Members' Groups and attend the annual members' conference and regional meetings. They also receive details of a wide range of gifts available by mail order or through RSPB shops.

For full details of membership and a free copy of the booklet *The Birds in Your Garden*, write to FREEPOST, Department 1878, at the above address.

COUNTY BIRD SOCIETIES

Check with your local library or see *The Birdwatchers Yearbook*, published annually by the Buckingham Press, Rostherne, Hall Close, Maids Moreton, Buckingham MK18 1RH.

II

Field Training Courses

The main provider of bird-oriented courses is the Field Studies Council, Preston Montford, Montford Bridge, Shrewsbury, Shropshire SY4 1HW. Write for information about activities at their widely-scattered field centres.

III

MAGAZINES

The longest-established and virtually indispensable magazine is the monthly *British Birds*. Lively but authoritative. Contact Erika Sharrock, Fountains, Park Lane, Blunham, Bedford MK44 3NJ for a free sample copy.

A relative newcomer to the field is *Bird Watching*, monthly from any newsagent. It contains details of latest sightings, equipment news, well-written and illustrated articles on every aspect of birding, readers' letters and all the usual magazine offerings. Good value and highly readable.

The newest, and most esoteric, contender in the magazine field is *Birding World*, which seeks to satisfy the thirst of the army of rarity hunters, whose role in birdwatching is so well illustrated elsewhere in this book by Peter Grant. Whether you regard twitching as a pure sport or as the cutting-edge of birding, this magazine is a vital ingredient. Subscription enquiries to Mrs H. Millington, Appletree Cottage, Marshside, Brancaster, King's Lynn, Norfolk PE31 8AD. With an address like that, the magazine has to be good . . .

And if you want the very latest in hotline information, dial BIRDLINE on 0898 700222 and tap in to the grapevine at source. An additional telephone service – BIRDCALL (0898 700227) – offers a more general bird news service, including a migration update, information about bird reserves and so on. (Calls to both these numbers are charged at a higher than normal rate. Phone 0485 210349 for full details.)

IV

OPTICAL EQUIPMENT

See Jim Flegg's *Binoculars, Telescopes and Cameras*, BTO Guide No. 14, from BTO, Beech Grove, Tring, Herts HP23 5NR.

And an excellent summary of current thinking, *Binoculars and Telescopes Survey*, price £1, from British Birds, Fountains, Park Lane, Blunham, Bedford MK44 3NJ.

V

BOOKS

Since there is a new bird book every week, you need to win the pools if you are going to have an exhaustive bird library. But *British Birds* magazine suggests that the following constitute the basic requirement.

CAMPBELL, B., LACK, E. *A dictionary of birds* Poyser, 1985.

CRAMP, S. *Handbook of the birds of Europe, the Middle East and North Africa: The birds of the Western Paleartic.*
Vols. 1–4 *Ostrich to ducks: Hawks to bustards; Waders to gulls; Terns to woodpeckers* OUP, 1978–85.

HEINZEL, H., FITTER, R. and PARSLOW, R. *The birds of Britain and Europe: with North Africa and the Middle East* Collins, new edn. pbk., 1972.

HOLLOM, P. A. D. *Popular handbook of rarer British birds* Witherby, 2nd rev. edn., 1980.

LACK, P. *The atlas of wintering birds in Britain and Ireland* Poyser, 1986.

PETERSON, R. *A field guide to the birds of Britain and Europe* Collins, 4th rev. edn., 1983.

SHARROCK, J. T. R. *The atlas of breeding birds in Britain and Ireland* Poyser, 1976.

VI

SUPPLIERS OF BIRD FURNITURE

RSPB, The Lodge, Sandy, Beds SG19 2DL. Catalogue.

Nerine Nurseries, Welland, Malvern, Worcs WR13 6LN. Bird tables, tit boxes, robin boxes, house martin nests.

Jamie Wood Ltd, Cross Street, Polegate, Sussex. Send for brochure.

VII

SUPPLIERS OF BIRD FOOD

E. W. Coombs Ltd, 25 Frindsbury Road, Strood, Kent.

John E. Haith Ltd, Park St, Cleethorpes, Lincs.

C. J. Wildbird Foods Ltd, The Rea, Upton Magna, Shrewsbury SY4 4UB. Seed, peanuts and the highly successful peanut germ which they market as 'Brambling brand granules'.

NEW SWOOP, a much improved version of the general garden bird mix, is available from all the obvious grocery and pet stores.

INDEX